THE LITTLE SCRIBE

By Ron Bateman

CON-PSY PUBLICATIONS MIDDLESEX

**First Edition
2004**

©Ron Bateman

Published by

CON-PSY PUBLICATIONS

**P.O. BOX 14,
GREENFORD,
MIDDLESEX, UB6 0UF.**

ISBN 1 898680 37 X

CONTENTS

The Little Scribe

A few words of explanation regarding the writings in this little volume. In March 2000, my life long friend and companion died, and soon afterwards I was "prompted" to sit down and write, and what I wrote surprised me. I was "told" via these writings that they would come from Brothers, who belong to what is known as "The White Brotherhood", and that they would work through Brian, (my companion), and that I was to be the last link in the chain as it were, for their Teachings. I am often awakened in the early hours and I go to my study and write quite quickly for about an hour, then I go back to bed and sleep. When I get up in the morning, I read what has been written and then record it on a cassette, then I listen to, and hopefully learn from what has been written. I am just the scribe and can take no credit for what is written, but I feel very privileged to be part of this on-going teaching, and am very grateful to my Brothers and Brian.

To those of you who have read this first little volume, I hope that words of comfort have helped you, and to those who are searching, I trust you have found what you were looking for.

May the Blessings of the One on High be with you now and always.

I dedicate this book to Brian, who is the inspiration for it, and to Irene, without whose help and encouragement this book could not have been written.

Thank you

Ron Bateman

"The Little Scribe"

Chapter 1

Welcome dear Brother in Christ Consciousness, we speak to you for a purpose.

In your mind you can travel to the far distant spheres, beyond the outer limits of your known Universe, to those unseen ones that lie beyond the perimeter of your visioned world! For the mind is not restricted or hampered by a gross form of existence, for it is beyond that restrictive environment called the Human Body! For the mind is timeless, and has always been, yes, even before the body that houses it! For The Mind is the Spiritual part of The Whole! For The whole, is Pure Spirit Matter, and that Matter is Mind! For without that capacity for Thought, where would your universes be? Still entombed within the silent world of Thought,-that slumbers! Until awakened by Divine Thought, or rather The Mind behind the thought. So you see Dear Little Brother, Thought, is Universal yes Universal, and if you think upon that phrase you will know that the word Universal means just what it says, a product of The Universe and what is that Universe? Why it is the visible body of The Almighty One known to many as God, The Creator!
So where does that leave us?! Why, we are part of that Universe, yes, even upon this planet of yours, it is part of the over all plan, the same as All forms of Living Matter is ! For the worlds that dwell within The Globe of Universal Love and Thought are all living breathing parts of that body of The One on High!

Mankind thinks to himself that God is a far off unseen unknown divinity, when in reality, He? It? is already within His grasp. For God is Now and within each and every living created being. Regardless of how you view the word "being" for being does not just mean Man himself, for being means a created entity, whether human, animal or even mineral! Think upon that and know that you are part of this great and wonderful achievement that we call God. Our minds or Spirits, or whatever you choose to call the force that illuminates an otherwise sterile form of life matter is from the one and only Source of All creation! This source, or shall we call it Force, for it is a force, a force of living growing matter that has it' origins in the Mind of The One on High that has been manifested into all living matter, and so you see little brethren upon the earth, we are all one, diverse, but never the less ,from the One Source of living energy. It is that energy force that is our life giving blood, and that blood is the very life force of The One on High Himself!

So think about what has been said, you are a part of but not the whole of The Universal Creator, and yet you have that Divine gift to create, not only yourselves but even the worlds to which you not only belong but inhabit! Think upon that and treat your Earth kindly, for if you don't, you are only harming yourselves! Your World, is but an infinitesimal fraction of the known and unknown universes. There are many, many, of you, and here we are speaking in terms of the Humanities, be they mankind or his unseen brothers, who dwell upon not only the distant spheres, but also within man himself! Think upon that also. We are All, part of each other, has that not occurred to you? We live, and have our being, because we are a part of each and everyone and everything that has ever been created, and is still being so! Remember friends, that Creation has never ever ceased, from the beginning till the End, creation will ever be! There are times when creation 'slumbers', still active, but formless, until the mind of The Creative Force is propelled into action once again , and so, more and more is created, and that not only goes for the various uninhabited worlds, but also those who will one day be it's inhabitants. And who will they be you wonder? You have always understood that Man as such is the supreme creation of The creator, but that need not be so, for The Creator always seeks to perfect that creation, and that can mean modification or re-adaptation of an existing species!

Do not think to yourselves, that you are the final outcome of God's creativity 'Oh no, you could be a blueprint for something even better! And more advanced than this primitive being who stands upright on his two legs and calls himself a 'Man' THINK, brethren, that you could be the forerunners for an even more wonderful form of so called 'mankind'? A creative Genius like The Almighty, would not be satisfied with just one attempt at creating a living thinking active creature, that can be endowed with all of His own God-like attributes, and yet who would know "himself" as part of that Divinity and behave accordingly! You and we, are just a small part of this ever on-going creativity, it is so vast, as to be incomprehensible to man, in his present state of evolution. There are others you know, who may look like man but have other attributes that would astonish the earthbound man, with his weak intellect as what he is really capable of! Mankind, that is the earth ones needs to be jolted out of his apathy, or torpor, and realise that he is just one of many, and yet all part of each other and, so you see we are all Brothers, even if we are not the same to behold. The Divinity has not stopped creating, how can He? For Creation is His very Life's blood! So, it is now up to man, to see himself, as a reflection of that Divine Principle,and endeavour to live like that Divine Principle, as he really knows within himself that he should.

The answer to all of Mans' problems , is his lack of love for his fellow creatures, and here we stress the word, creatures, for that word encompasses many creations, and not just man. Once he starts to think of

6

others, before he thinks of himself, then he will really start to live as "God" intends him to, and will begin to fulfil what the "Almighty Ones" have sought to bring to fruition upon this dense planet of yours called Earth. Try to remember, that you are not the only man-like creation in this part of your Universe, and then think, if there are others like us, what will happen when we come face to face? Will we be able to compare ourselves favourably with them, or will we be ashamed of our lack of just the basic qualities that we have been endowed with? Think, and start to try and live in the right and proper manner. You know the remedy for all of your so-called ills, which unfortunately you seem to bring upon yourselves.

Learn to live in Harmony with your surroundings, do not fight with them, live wisely and justly and then you will begin to realise that this earth of yours is not such a bad place after all.But it will take discipline and sacrifice if you want to change your world for the better! Make a start now! Don't leave it to others who may follow you, give them a world that they can live in Peace and harmony with, and not the devastated planet that we can see becoming more and more unhappy as each day passes.

Chapter 2

There has always been much speculation, regarding those other worlds that exist out there in space. Your scientists view them, that is the ones that they have given names to, and they wonder about whether they can sustain life such as what you have upon this your earth-plane of existence. They only see what they think they see, when in reality there are far more planets there than can be seen with your physical eyes. In other words Dear friend, they are invisible, and yet they really do exist -but not in your dimension! Their vibrations are so far advanced as to render them as being unseen , by those upon your world, and yet they are visible to other planets that are on the same vibrationary wavelengths as their own. Now you think to yourself ,what about those inhabitants -if there are any, are they real or imaginary?? Well dear friends they do exist, just as you do. They are as it were, just as solid in their own way, as you appear to be! For in truth, you upon the earth, if seen from afar would perhaps be as unseen beings to their perception! You notice we say -"perception" that should give you a clue as to what we mean. They perhaps see you, but not with their eyes,-that should make you think! If not with their eyes then, what with? Other species can "see " with their whole body, if you wish to call the life force by that name! We will say 'body', for that word you can understand. The word "lifeforce" though true, does not allow you any room for thought as to what that truly means! Lifeforce is pure energy it is made up of fine very very fine molecules, of what you would term 'electrical currents' and when these currents are assembled in their right order they form what you would call 'a body'! You also are made up of electrical currents , but you are unaware of their true potential. Man has as yet not been 'programmed' to understand how he can manipulate these currents to his own advantage! When he has progressed sufficiently, then he will have his' inner eyes ' opened, so that he can be taught by those who are more advanced than him. But that, dear friends is a long way off in your earth time scale. Upon earth your vibrations are somewhat restricted, it is like living in a form of what you would call-"soup"! You are sluggish, your whole body is heavy and difficult to manipulate, you have to rely upon physical exertion to not only move, but also to create the means for food intake to keep that body in an active state.

Others in your Universe do not have to rely upon "physical exertion" for these things. They can and do, everything with their thought waves. You upon earth use your thinking cells in a very amateur way, you have absolutely no idea of what real thought is capable of! When you do finally comprehend what "true thought" is all about, you will look back upon these times as a very very primitive form of existence! As we have pointed out, your realm is of a dense form of life force and is not yet in it's pure state. This is all for a specific purpose, the body that your 'real' self inhabits is for you to try and understand the basic principles of what life is for. And it is not what you imagine it to be! When in your" pure state" of original life force, you have no idea of your capabilities or even of who or what you are! You are as it were a 'jelly like' substance, unfinished as it were, waiting for the mind substance to animate it into activity, in other words bring it into a living form of existence, where it can learn to understand what "it is" that "it is"! But for that to come about it has to be shall we say, born or created into a form of substance that can allow it to make 'judgments' and try to make sense of those judgments. In other words, learn what life is supposed to be about. That is but one way the amoeba form of life is brought into existence! Not all forms are of the 'man-like' substance of existence !That is not to say that they do not resemble what you would term a physical type of body -like being. They do and are, but they are of a finer essence, they have not had to start from what we would call the basic life form, which is you little people of the earth!

There are many ways of not only learning, but also returning to the primitive force of original material substance that is your original Self. Much for you to think about is it not, dear friends? We, that is all forms of physical like beings, and that is a very loose term for you to understand, are all from the same Mould. But as it were created by -shall we call them 'different creative Beings of Light.' That is why there are different forms of creative beings or structures that you think of as the "humanities". That implies that you are just one of many of these shall we say, 'varieties' in existence. What a lot of re-thinking for you isn't there? But it is necessary if you are to learn, and progress forever upward back to your Source of Creation. You do not have to remain all of your lives as a physical type being, of human-like structure. As you progress you are allowed to take on different structures, that suit your particular environment in your constant evolutionary cycles! We started off this discourse telling you of the other worlds that exist , whether they can be observed by you upon the earth or not, and now you know that the inhabitants where applicable are not exactly the same as yourselves and yet you are all the same basically. And now you should be able to as it were 'get on' with each other, when the time comes for that to come about.

The whole of the lives that you lead are for that purpose, to know and be known. You are all part of the Creative principles! Take note of that word principles! If you think correctly you will comprehend what we are saying! You upon the Earthplane have a long way to go before you can be assimilated into the body of the true creative understanding of what that form of creation is all about.

9

Chapter 3

We will try to enlighten you regarding some of those other spheres of existence that are a reality, but not in the same sense as your world is. That no doubt makes you wonder if they are not the same as us, how do they differ? Well Dear friend, for a start they vibrate at a much higher rate than your earth, and that means that they cannot be visualised by your earth eyes, or even your advanced telescopes, for their orbits do not correspond to yours! Difficult for you to comprehend. Try and imagine a large large sphere, or if you wish, a globe. Fill it with water and what do you see? Nothing? And yet that water is teeming with life, yes even a drop under a microscope would show you a tiny world of creatures, all alive and thriving.Well, imagine then that you or rather your world and others are in a vast vast empty globe, but in reality it is not empty, it just appears so to those "worlds" that are vibrating at different rates, some you will be able to observe, others will not be able to be viewed by your so-called sense of seeing. But tune in to these other vibrations with your inner senses, and you will be amazed at what else you can perceive. Not real, and yet-very much so, to those who are inhabiting those 'unseen' spheres! Much for you to ponder on little scribe.

The worlds' or spheres that we speak of are realities, even if you at present cannot observe them. Once you 'travel' to a higher sphere, that is when you have left your body's shell behind you, you will then begin to vibrate at a higher velocity and so you will be "in tune", not only with your surroundings but also with those who dwell upon them. For you are now not only a part of that new world, but you "are", that new world! Think upon that and see if you can come to the right conclusion. When we 'transmit' to a higher plane of thought, we actually become part of that living organism.We are what we perceive! Difficult for you to understand? Even upon your earth, you are if you did but know it part of that earth, that life force that goes to make and keep it existing. You perhaps have not realised it, but collectively all people are part of the living structure of where they are at any given moment. Without 'us', and that does not mean 'us', but you, universally, there would be no living planet, just a sterile 'wilderness'. It is the various life forms and that includes Man, that brings to life what was just a sterile form of existence. So you see little friend, we are all important to where we find ourselves dwelling. To live, and learn how to live, and that means studying others in the process, that way we learn how to proceed further up the scale of Evolution, towards The God Head, that we know one day we will aspire to, and hopefully attain that perception of not only purity, but of Universal love and understanding.

Do not think about that part for the present, for it is a long long way off, not only for you dear friends, but even for us, and yes, even those above us. Perfection, is an illusive form of knowledge, one that has many sides to it's perception, and with each incarnation, and here we do not refer to the earth planet, with each upward incarnation, so we perceive another dimension of what Perfection is all about. What you upon earth would term perfection, would upon another planet be deemed imperfect! Lessons to be learned, all is not what it appears to be. so much of our 'lives' are illusions of one sort or another, and that goes for the Higher forms of living as well as for your gross earth-plane. And 'illusion' is still an 'illusion'! Think of that! For what is 'illusion' to one, is a' reality' to another! And yet even within the reality there dwells a form of illusion, does there not? Much thinking for you to do dear friends, much thinking. Remember, think and observe for "yourselves", do not accept everything even what we have to say- at face value. It is not wrong to question, for when you do, then your mind is opening up. We have had to learn the hard way, just as you are. Question Question Question, and make sure that the answers that you get stimulate your little thinking machine, and learn from it, and then question again. For learning can only be achieved by asking, and asking will help you to understand, even if at first you find some of the answers that you receive are somewhat bewildering and maybe ambiguous! For the answers are given to stimulate your thought patterns and to jolt you out of what might appear to others, as apathy! DO NOT BE CONTENT. Always seek further and you will get the answers that will satisfy you, and -yes- help you to progress on the upward trail of knowledge and understanding. We feel that we will leave our discourse there, for there is much for you to assimilate and think over. But remember it is you, who must ultimately come to what you feel, is the right conclusion. Do not take our word for it. Think for yourselves, and in the thinking you will find the answers that you seek.

Chapter 4

Long long ago it was not thought permissible to question either the teachings of The Holy Bible or even those who's job it was to translate it into everyday meanings, but today, it is quite quite different, it is actually encouraged, and so today people are somewhat sceptical of what has always been thought of as sacrosanct! Well this of course has resulted in a lot of misunderstanding. Some people have discarded the teachings and their inner meanings and have indulged themselves in various alternative life styles, thinking to themselves they are being very clever and modern! In fact some have even gone further, and questioned the very source of All Creation! How foolish they are, for can they put anything concrete in the place of what they wish to discard? No! it would seem that their feeble explanations cannot stand up to investigation and so they are left somewhat in a vacuum, and when in that state, they are liable to be influenced by what we shall call in laymen's' terms "Religious cranks!" It would seem that the word 'religion' draws people like a magnet to all forms of cults and dubious creeds. None of which can stand up to the test of time!

Man has been endowed with a brain, complex and wonderful, and a mind to electrify that organ into activity, but it is a two edged sword, for unless he knows how to control it he is left floundering. Man is right to question, but he must do it with not only an "open mind" but with sincerity. The whole concept of Creation and The Creator, has to be carefully evaluated, and not only discussed, but even when it does not seem feasible it is up to him to look within and ask himself for guidance! You notice we have said -"ask himself for guidance",-and not God! That will make you sit up and say ,Who then can we ask for guidance -if not God? Have you not grasped that you are God, and so you are your own investigator and teacher! People will shudder at that thought, and some will even cry blasphemy! Well, we are not dwelling in the middle ages, you cannot put people on the rack for questioning the very existence of the one you term as God! Heresy is only a matter of words , and is used to try and cover up what a thinking person is trying to understand and explain. So as the idea of a Human-like Creator and the actual Creation cannot be verifiable in laymen's' terms, they put it to one side and call out -'heresy'!

Creation can never be fully explained to the man in the street, and yes, even to those who profess to know how it all came about! They have "no idea". They have theories, and that is all, and what may be thought of as "gospel" today, in a hundred years or less hence, the whole conception will be turned upside down with more theoretical explanations! Man as such, can never be expected to fully understand all of the mysteries of Creation. The mysteries of the Creation of this Universe of His, that is the one to which he lives and tries to observe! Think upon that little people of the Earth. For there is more to your so called universe than you can ever imagine! And you notice we have said "your Universe" and do you understand the meaning of the word "your"? For if you do you will know that there are more than one Universe! And "they" are not yet visible or knowable to you upon this little planet of yours! You look at Space and try to look into it, and yet you do not see what is there, only what you think you see! What Space holds is forever changing. What you observe today has long disappeared so you can never be sure of what is that you are actually seeing! For you are looking at it with your eyes and not those that are within! And we speak not of the orbs of sight! Look with the inner sight! And that does not mean sight! Man at this stage of his development cannot be expected to fully understand all the intricacies of creation. For creation has never ceased. It is forever on-going and so as such is an unknowable force that will never be able to be explained to his own satisfaction. He thinks he can tamper with it and be a creator in his own right! Never! This aspect of man has not been programmed for that kind of work. Look around you and see what a mess you are making of this your world of existence! So how could you possibly be endowed with that creative principle? You would abuse it in no time! You are but puppets in the hands of The Creators, and think about that! "Creation is thought made manifest!" You can never take on that mantle, you are but Thoughts of the Creative Principle, not the Creative Principle itself, remember that before you discard what you have and seek what is someone else's! And that "someone" need not be of or from your known world of existence. You are but one of many forms of creative thought. Think about that also, and know, that you have much to learn about yourselves before you can learn about other life forms that do exist, even if not yet observable to you!

Man must look within, and look as if he is looking from without! In other words, dispassionately. You are not what you observe with your outward vision, you are more complex than that. You are many, and yet you are one, more for you to think about, as is the Creator of all Creations! The life of the Universe has been ordered and in time will have altered, for that is the way of All Creation! It never stands still for if it did, then chaos would ensue. Creation defies explanation, at least to man in his present state. For what is explanation today is unexplainable tomorrow. Cease your probings into the unknown for if you were to find what you think you are looking for, you would not be able to accept it. You have not yet explored your own intelligence to see if you would be able to interpret what you may come into contact with. There is so much you need to know about yourselves and your place in the scheme of things, for you do have a place believe us, but that place has not yet been given to you, you are still on probation. Think upon that also. Probation and all that that word means.

Chapter 5

We will begin this chapter with the words "Trust in The Lord" your God! For in Him you can put your whole trust and know that He will not forsake you ever. So many people pay lip service to God and leave it at that, hoping that that is sufficient, but it is not. For lip service alone is not the answer, for it is actions that speak louder than words. That does not imply that you have to try and think ,'how can I please God, what shall I do to make Him notice me?' God does not require you to tell Him what you think He ought to do! For to Him all things are known before they are even thought of. We think that if we talk and I say "talk", because that is what the majority of people do when they think that they are at their prayers! Do you think that He needs reminding all the time what we think we need? For most of the time that is spent in prayer is not for the benefit of others but for self. We do as it were, sublimate ourselves to God, we are here to entreat Him to look kindly upon us and then give us what we ask! Do you think that God is some sort of Supermarket, where all the things that you think you need are there for the asking? When you pray, you should as it were shut yourself into a quiet room, which is the one inside yourself, and then just be quiet and listen to the small voice that is ever present within you and let it do the talking, which you will find is just the inner silence that is all that is necessary, for it is God that dwells within that inner voice and knows just what it is that you need, yes need, not desire. Have you not noticed that how often your so-called prayers of supplication do NOT receive the answer that you think you warrant? God cannot be mocked, and though that is not your intention, it is in reality, for you are telling God what you think He should do, not what He wants for your welfare.

Silence is the greatest of all forms of prayer, or conversations with The Almighty. For in the silence an answer is given, to your unspoken thoughts. THINK, before you embark upon your desire for communion with Him, Peace, and stillness of voice is all that is required for God to know what it is that is needed for a quiet mind. If only people would cease their verbal babble, and just give themselves up to the quietness of a still- like mind and let the flow of God's love embrace them, cleansing them of all their fears and longings. Refresh yourselves with His everlasting LOVE, which is there in abundance if you could only realise it.

Have you not noticed that when you enter an empty church or cathedral that the stillness is overwhelming, you bathe in that stillness and feel not only refreshed but actually nearer to your Maker. When the church is full then the stillness is lost, for the mundane thoughts of the congregation are like a multitude of sounds, and the stillness is dissipated. When you enter a house of God you are a visitor, and as such you should respect the dwelling place of The One on High, and that respect is shown by stilling those thoughts that you have unwittingly brought along with you. Before entering that hallowed dwelling place, you should pause, and mentally cast aside all those thoughts, and enter with a contrite heart and a desire to meet your God in pure silence. Listen to what He Tells You and not what you wish to tell Him! You will say "Well if we don't voice our thoughts how will He know what we want? " You see, "what we want"! When it should be 'What is it Father, that you wish me to do?'

The next time you visit your place of worship, go in with a still voice, do not let your mind distract you. Just be still and listen to the Silence, that stillness that is all embracing. You go to your place of worship to be united with God, let Him into your very heart, by being quiet in your mind. Cast aside all the worries and thoughts of the days that have gone, and give yourselves up to the Peace of that hallowed place. Yet, you ARE that hallowed place if you did but know it, For You are the Temple wherein God dwells, you are His dwelling place, listen to Him, live with Him and for Him, and that means loving one another without any reservations, and that love should encompass All religions, there should be no distinctions. For God is everywhere and within everyone regardless of their form of worship! Religion, if practised as it was intended, should be a balm for the worried soul, and not a barrier to friendship. Look upon your neighbour or whoever you encounter as the fellow traveller along the pathway to God. He is within us all-never forget that, if only we could learn to see Him in everything we do.

Remember you are The temple of god. You are his Building, treat yourself as a holy person and do unto others what you would wish them to do to you! We are all brothers and sons of the one Father, look kindly upon each other, do not judge another person because of their colour or their looks, for they too are temples of God, and should be treated as such. Learn to Live and let live. God is UNIVERSAL, and that means just what it says, Universal, He is not confined to one place or even to one form of so-called Religious culture! Put aside your old thoughts and start afresh! God is Everywhere and within All of Life! Try to see the other person's point of view. Cast off the trappings of different cultures and see that within them dwells The Eternal God of All Creation. Yes, within us all. So when you judge another you are in fact judging yourself if you did but know it!

Think, upon these thoughts, and then enter the stillness of your soul and know that God is God, and no other. In other words, you are He and He is you. Accept that fact and believe as you really know you should, however hard that may be at times, if you can only see the God within the other person then you will have achieved what God intended you to do. LOVE ONE ANOTHER. Start now,do not judge, just try and understand, and in the stillness of your heart, you will know that you are trying to do God's Work for in another's face, you are beholding your very own, -Which is GOD'S!

Chapter 6

Yes dear Brother we do wish to talk with you, and may what we wish to say to you be of not only interest to you but also as blessings as well! We will start with the words 'Our Lord and Master Jesus the Christ', for it is in His name that we come to you, and through His name that we exist, For we are known as The White Brotherhood of Christ. Yes dear friend, we are all bound by that name and in His service we endeavour to not only help but also teach what He had to impart to mankind all those Earth years ago. For that wisdom that He left us, is ageless and is just as important to the right way of living today, as it was then. Man has not changed, he will always need a leader to look up to, and show him the way. But in reality he needs no one but himself, for within his bosom dwells the Spirit Essence of that Divine One you all call Christ, sent by his -and your Father, to be an example of what is expected of His children and what they can achieve if only they listen to that inner voice of consciousness that is, The Living Christ within all of us. Did He not say when He was about to leave this Earth, 'I leave with you The Holy Spirit that will dwell within, in you forever'. That was the promise He made that was given to Him by Our Father, so that all of his children could become Christ's, not only in thought but in reality.

But dear brethren, what has become of that legacy that He bequeathed to us? Have we lost it? Have we abandoned those words that he spoke, "Love ye one another", "Do unto others as you would be done by". The precepts for a right and righteous life of service to not only God, but to mankind himself. Where are those memories? Do we not use them anymore? Are we so bound up by our own selfish desires that those inner thoughts are pushed way way back so that we can hardly remember that they ever existed! Jesus our dear brother was the Brother of us all, and believe us, still is, wherever the name is uttered. For The Christ Spirit that dwelt within that mortal body is very much alive today and not only in what you call 'your World'. For He is not confined to just one planet of existence, He or rather His Teachings and examples are in very truth Universal. They go under many names, and many so-called religious cultures, but nevertheless they remain the same. They are the very thoughts of The One on High made manifest, in the flesh of the one called Jesus, and that dear friends means you and me in fact all of us, for we are all one and the same, and our name is engraved upon our very soul, and that name is Christ, and the manifested Spirit that we call Jesus, who is you and me, all of humanity. We are the products of that divine body who is the "Jesus Man". We cannot separate ourselves from Him for His Spirit, the one divine gift that The One on High

16

bestowed upon Him who He called "My Son", for he meant not just the man called Jesus, but all of mankind. We could all be called Jesus if we did but know it. For Jesus was not just the one man, He is All men!

Think upon that statement and know that it is The Truth. We are all from the one Creator of all Life. Cast aside your thoughts of what your seekers of knowledge tell you about the Creation of The Universe, they speak to you in riddles, for they know not the Thoughts of the One on High, and The Universe is but one of those thoughts made as it were, flesh wherein we dwell. For God, or The Creator is not only Universal, He Is the Universe.

We are part of that body, that lives and breathes and has it's life force from His very own breath! We are children of His Thought, and through His Thoughts we have what we call Life, it is but a little piece of what is endless and unknowable, and yet it is known, just look around you, see your brethren, see the trees, the birds of the air, the fish of the sea, the animals that roam the land. They are you and you are them! Yes, we are all part of the body of the One Creator The unknowable One you call God because you desire to have a name in which to call upon when terror threatens you. But God, as you call The Creator is within you all the time and is striving to make Himself known to you. Listen, listen to that inner voice, that you try to still, you never can, for it is the voice of Him who is our Brother, our Sister, our Mother, our Father, OUR GOD; wake up to your inheritance that He has bequeathed unto you namely, that Christ Spirit that is everlasting and never dies! The body may wither and even disappear, but the Spirit within will forever be alive and a part of Him who created thee and breathed His very breath into the life form that inhabits not only this little world but All Worlds, and the word 'World' can mean many things including man himself..

You are a living cosmos. You are the face of the One who is faceless, the One who is known and yet unknown. Look within and see who it is that dwells within this body you call mortal man! What can you see? Do you recognise the face that appears to you? Do you see the One who is your Brother? The Jesus man who gave His own life in service to mankind that man may one day approach the throne upon High, and be once more reunited in The Body of The Creator of all Life! We are born to live and learn, and to learn just who we really are,- and who is that? You have no need to ask for you already know that you are GOD and GOD is YOU. If you really can believe that, then you will start to live as you know God wishes you to. For you are the children of The One God, and as His children you are part of His very body, the Universal body of the whole of Creation. We all depend upon each other, even when we pretend we do not need another's helping

17

hand. Look upon your neighbour not only as your brother but also a manifested Spirit of the One on High! In fact, yourself in reverse! Your brother is the face in the mirror that you see but cannot see, for you only observe the outward appearance of what you call, man, when within that shell there shines a force that were you to be able to see it, would blind you with it's radiance! Yes dear friends we are speaking not only to you, but of you. You are that spark of The Divinity, Let it shine forth! Let it be a beacon on the Hilltop for all to see! Brothers in Christ you are, learn to see your Brother in everything that you do. Love one another as you should love yourself, then you will have learnt how to truly Live! Remember we are all Brothers no matter the race, the colour, or the so-called religion! Religion, when properly lived as it was intended to be, can be a force for good, and not a stumbling block to global unity! For God, acknowledges NO Religion as The ONE Religion, -that is man's small thinking. God, is beyond that concept of what man chooses to call 'his God'. God is no ones, and yet He is everyone's and so man is bound by that law, and until he understands that, he will never find the Peace either within himself or with others that he seeks. You are the Universal face of The One on High, the Unknowable One who is yet the Known One that dwells within Us All.

When next you behold your face in the mirror, look deeply and see the face of not the one who is looking, but the one who is behind the seen eyes, and then say to yourself, 'I have seen the Face of God', and then strive to be like Him. It is not too late for mankind to think again of what Jesus said all those millenniums ago. "LOVE ONE ANOTHER" and in loving one another, you are loving your God, you are loving yourself, for you are God, even if it's just a small part of Him and you know it not.

We leave you in Peace and may the Blessings of that One upon High be with you and within you from this day forward and forever more. Peace, Peace, and may you release The Christ Spirit within your breast and begin to Live as you know you should.

Chapter 7

Truth in all it's aspects! And what is it that we call the Truth? Is it the truth that we are made in the image of our God? Is it a truth that we are three in one? Nay we are more than that! Is it a truth that within this shell called a body dwells one called Spirit? Are these all aspects of the one Truth? And are there more? We say unto you Yes! There are, but we are not permitted to show unto you the full volume of those truths, for they would be too much for you to comprehend. Be content with just a few, and those that are called 'The mysteries of life' will be shown to you when you are ready to receive them and not before.

What truth shall we speak of tonight? You ask "Jesus", well, so be it. The Nazarene has always been an enigma to man, and as such will remain so for the time being. You wonder at that statement! Yes you are right to question, Jesus, and here we speak not of the man but of the Spirit within, that has been designated as the "Christos", that aspect of the One on High that is unknowable and yet is known by one and all! Yes, by one and all, we repeat that statement, for the Christos is not only Universal, He is all men! "It" is that part of The Creator of all things that dwells within each and every human being, yea and in those above the realms of the Earth and even those realms of the Spirit, where dwell those who you call Angels. Some are or have been mortals, others have never touched the Earth-plane as living entities and yet there are those who not only dwell in the Land of the Spirit, but do come down from a higher plane of knowledge. These are Truths little scribe, write them down! You seek to know the riddle of life,-that is simple! Live within and not without of the body you call mortal, for in truth you are a spark of the One who is Immortal! He has been and will be forever the One who is the Unknowable One! But you question, why unknowable? Well little friend, do you know yourself? Well do you? The answer must be 'no'. We are not programmed to know all things, just sufficient to make us want to know more. Will we ever know all those things that we search for? The answer to that question is NOT in the life time of the body upon Earth. For Earth is but a playground of the Spirit! And do not misunderstand what we say! For the Earth is the training ground for the Spirit to learn, and in the learning aspire to know even more. In that way, you are growing evermore like the One that dwells within you as a spark of the Divine.

You now ask about the man whom you know as Jesus, well little person ask! Yes, He was and is real! He was a flesh and blood human being, just as you are, with the exception that he knew exactly who and what He was, and why He had been chosen to be a vehicle of the Divine Principle. He grew in stature to manhood, not only pure in mind and body, but with the

19

inner understanding of what was to befall His mortal body. Not as has been told you as a lamb to the slaughter, but as a willing participant in God's plan. Understand, dear brethren of the Earth, God works in mysterious ways, His Knowledge to impart! The vehicles He chooses are ones that are relevant to the times. So, cease looking for the Second Coming, for it is here already and has always been! Look not to the future, look within yourselves. There you will find the answer that you seek! Do you understand the meaning of what we have said? Think about it, We are here to help you learn about yourself but we cannot do it for you. The Christos dwells within all of US! Yea on whatever sphere of existence we find ourselves dwelling. So then, where is this Second Coming coming from? Have you not realised that it is within you?? You, that is ALL Mankind are the aspects of the second Coming! It is up to YOU to make that happen! Don't sit back and wait for a revelation to hit you! For it will not, however long you wait for it to happen. You are the Revelation! Your "God" is You, and you are your GOD. It is up to man to make of his life what God has intended for him. But man must do this for himself, he cannot expect another to do it for him! You have had your Master and Teacher who gave to you the Truths from on high, to live and prosper by. Do not blame Him if you have not taken heed of what He said. For what was given to you all those centuries ago, still holds good in today's lifetime. But, are those precepts lived by? No, we say, and again we say No! that is why your Earth is in such a sorry state! You have not yet learned the lessons that that One gave to you. "Love ye one another" "Honour your Father and Mother" "Give to the poor" and in doing so you enrich yourself. Nay, not the physical, the Spiritual, is what we talk of! You are made up of Spirit! Live in and through that 'other' you. Think not of so-called Earthly values, they are but tinsel that flies away in the wind, look for the stability that is within you, bring it to the fore. Learn to live for one another, look in the mirror of life and behold not your brother but yourself! You are your brother and he is you. We are all one, and come from the ONE, who is The creator of all life! Be like "Him" for in truth you are Him, can you not see that? When you do, then you will know who you really are, not this little figure that struts upon the stage of life and thinks of itself as God. For though he is, he does not really believe that, for if he did then this world would become a part of Heaven and not what it is at present,- a poor reflection of what it could be.

Think dear friends, think, go into the Silence of your mind and listen to what is said to you, and then try to live by what is given to you. That is one of the Truths that you are searching for, and it already dwells within you! Release that Spirit within listen to it's voice, for it is the voice of reason. It is the voice of GOD.

20

Chapter 8

Think upon the words that were uttered so long ago by the one you call Jesus. The gospels give you many quotations of that One, and yet- are they lived up to in this day and age? And yea, were they even adhered to even then? Mankind is a strange creature, he asks for help and then ignores it, and why? Because he thinks that he knows best! But his thoughts are jumbled up and he does not think coherently! He is perverse, and why should that be you ask? Is it because deep down he thinks he knows best and prefers to stumble along in the dark, instead of holding his head high into the Light. Look back and you will see that man has always been like this, and is today so what is it that holds him back from striding forth into the Light of reason and understanding? Is it this "freewill" that we hear so much about? Yea, that is just an excuse for his wayward behaviour! The freedom to think for himself has long been his excuse, but there comes a time when he can no longer use that excuse. He must turn back to God and the scriptures and not only read them but learn from them! They were given to him as a guide for right living, and if he had adhered to those principles his world of today would be a different place to live in. All forms of Religious culture have guidelines for their followers and if you were to compare them you would find so many similarities that you would be forgiven for thinking that they must have all come from the One Source, and you would be right, - They have! So why is it that man ignores this fact? When if he really lived up to those ideals he would learn to understand not only his fellow man but also his God, and his God is the God of all! And not just one clan. However much that particular clan thinks of itself as the one and only one that has the ear of God! If they really listened then they would understand that we all spring from the same source! We are all the same fundamentally, we may not all look alike, or for that matter think alike, but that should not be a barrier to understanding each other. It is Greed that is the motivating force that tears man apart. Greed not only of the body but the Spirit also. If man really wants to live in peace and harmony he must first change his outworn ideas of just who and what he is. He has been given this world to make of it a Heaven! And not a wilderness as he seems bent on doing. He digs up this earth and concrete's it over to build even more ugly edifices to satisfy his own desires, instead of cultivating the land upon which he dwells. The way he is going about it , there will be no land to cultivate for the nourishment he needs to sustain his life's blood. Then what will he do? Manufacture synthetic food stuff, that will not only dull his brain but eventually disintegrate his very body! You have been given all the necessary forms of life -giving organisms to sustain a healthy

21

body and mind. Why are you frittering it away with substitutes for a healthy diet? Learn to live with nature and not against her, she provides you with everything you need, but you are trying to turn her into a factory of disease and not of health! Why do you think you have so much dissatisfaction these days? Because you have lost the basic desire to live in harmony with the natural resources and seek to control what you cannot! For Nature, is another word for God, and He will Not be mocked by man, Believe us!

You think you make progress, but do you? Think about it, Why have you so much unhappiness in your world today? It is because you have lost your way not only physically but spiritually as well! The two are one, and cannot be separated. Feed the Spirit and then you will understand how to feed the body! You think the wrong way round! It is the Spirit that should be the guiding force for the body. Once you learn to live not only for Spirit but by Spirit also, then you will have learned the lesson of why, you are here in the first place. Give of your Spirit to those in need, and not only to feed the body! And we mean give freely-with No restrictions as to how they should live their own lives! Religion, should Not - come into it! Practice what you preach, do not preach what you do not practice! One day Religion will be a thing of the past, for all mankind will know who their GOD is, for they will know that they are not only an aspect of that One on High, but that they are, that One! Much to think upon! If you can believe that, then you are on the right track to being what it is that God has created you for. Do not isolate yourselves from each other , but then again, do not impose your way of thinking upon them either! Learn to live in toleration with all of your brethren. Man is Not an island, he is a Continent made up of many! Learn your lessons and learn them well before it is too late! You are not God yet, you may think you are, but you have a long, long, way to go before you can assume that Title!

We leave you to think carefully about what has been said, and then act upon it! You do have the ability to change for the better, start now, and see how your lives will alter, bring back LOVE into your living, for it is only through LOVE that you will be able to achieve what it is that will really make a difference to the way you live.

Chapter 9

The journey of life or rather, we should say the journey of Lives that we take to reach the goal that has been set us, is a journey not only of the body and that word encompasses the many bodies that we inhabit when setting out upon this voyage of discovery, and that voyage is to discover just who we are and not who we think we are! We sometimes get confused as to just who we feel we are! That is shall we say quite understandable, because we start out these voyages as one identity, that to all intents and purposes is the real 'I' so why should we bother to look for another one? When it takes us all our time looking after the one that we are inhabiting on this Earth! But then we are somewhat -shall we say, "blinkered", for one life at a time seems quite enough to be going on with, without the added encumbrance of another that we are not quite sure of!

But then this "other body" is shall we say a safety net, in case the inhabited one is in need of it! And if we did but realise it, that one is the important one and not the other way around! If we can begin to see that this other one is the one who governs this Earthly one and carries it along as it were through it's Earthly journey, then we would be a far happier and complete being, instead of the one that is continually searching for the reason of why we are even here! We are told that it is to learn the lessons of life to fit us for the future ones, but just what is it that these 'lessons' teach us? Is it how to be a better person? And what does that encompass?! Being kind to one another? Not being selfish? Looking after those who are in need? Yes, all of these lessons are worthwhile and should make of us better people but do they? So often those so-called virtues are used not to benefit others but to further the ambitions of the one who practises them! You may think that that seems a harsh judgment but if you stop to think about it, just how many people that you know really are such true and altruistic beings? It seems that this life instead of bringing out the best in a person seems to encourage, not shall we say the worst, but at the best indifference to what this life is really all about, or rather should be about! You will argue, that this life is a hard one, and that a person must look out for themselves first and others later! Well we grant you it may appear that that is the way most people have to live their lives, but is it the right way? We so often fall short of our intended purposes to try and be better than we are! So is that one of the lessons that we have to learn? Surely the answer is Yes! But how to go about it? For this life seems so cruel and the expression "Dog eat Dog" is the one that expresses it! But that only perpetuates this form of unhappiness within our soul!

If we can look upon each other as not just a brother but also a friend, then perhaps we can begin to live a life of Service, which benefits not only others but also ourselves! -If we did but know it! You can put others first and still look after yourselves, it can be done but it needs to be worked at! This life upon this planet Earth is but a training ground, not just for the body but mainly for the Spirit within! For that is the one that will go on living when this earthly one has shed it's shell and starts once more upon the Spiritual path of evolution! So, you see those so-called lessons that we are here to learn, are important, they are what makes the Spirit grow and prepare itself for the next stage in it's journey ever upward! We tend to think of Spirit as something that one day we will become, instead of realising that we are Spirit here and now ,not something in the future! This body that we inhabit, is but a cloak of identity whilst we tarry upon this plane of existence. It is the Spirit that is the reality not this outward show that we call ourselves. If mankind can think of himself first as Spirit and then as human-like body, then perhaps he will be able to not only learn the lessons of life but will be able to conquer them more easily than he does. Instead of striving for this life he should be thinking of the one to come which is the permanent one, and not this transient one that takes him all of his earth time to complete! You may think that all sounds very fine in theory, but we are here upon this Earth and as such we have to fight to exist! Granted, that is what it seems like, but it should not be a fight, it should be a joy. If man can learn to live and let live and yes, understand what it is that makes others behave in the way they do, then he can live the way it is intended that he should! Tolerance, in all things. Don't try to outdo your neighbour, it really is not worth it in the long run is it? If we could all try to live as one big family and not fight amongst ourselves, then this world of yours would be more like the Heaven we think that one day we will inhabit! It can be the NOW, and not in the future. Lessons need not be hard -when you see them for what they are! They are just stepping stones along the path that leads us to the fuller life that we will inhabit after we have left this one behind us! We all seem to look forward to that one as if it is a reward for all the trials and tribulations of the Earth one, yet if we learn to live as we should, then this Earth one would be far more tolerable and livable than we seem to expect it to be! Life should be one of joy and happiness, not one of continual strife, we are here to try and make of this earth a forerunner of our life in the hereafter, Heaven if you wish to call it that! Heaven can be here and now, we have the ingredients to make of this Earth one if we only try, it may mean sacrifice and that really means not putting ourselves first all the time! But it will be worth it, you will see smiling faces and not the frowning ones that seem to be the norm these days! Start to live for one another, share what you have, keep enough for yourselves, but any surplus should be given freely to those in need. Make this whole world a heaven of plenty, for there really is enough to go round and to spare! Just make sure that it is shared, and not hoarded as it is at present! Your world can be a wonderful place in which to live and learn, that is what it is intended to be, not the war driven planet that we see it is heading for. STOP! Take a long look at yourselves and change your mode of thinking before it is too late! Cultivate your Earth first and then you can think about what it is in space that seems to intrigue you. Put your own house in order, and then perhaps you may get visitors who wish to see you and not feel apprehensive at what they now observe! Think upon these things, for it is your life that we are talking about -not ours! We bid you farewell and pray that your eyes may be opened and your hearts also!

Chapter 10

Let us start with the words "Knock and the door shall be opened for you." Words that convey an inner meaning to one who is open minded and who is searching for the Truth! For truth comes in many guises and is not always apparent as the truth, it is only perhaps later that one realises that what one is searching for, is already in one's possession! Life is one long search for that illusive truth, each day presents another facet of it, if you are looking for it! So often it lies beneath our very noses and still we are not aware of it! The answer is, not to search, for the truth will present itself to you when you are ready to receive it. So now we will look at the truth that is so illusive and yet is so obvious to us if we did but realise it!

The fundamental Truth is to Love One Another, with what is termed 'The Universal Love' of all mankind! And yes, also those brothers of his in the Animal Kingdom. For all of life stems from the One on High and so is our brother in truth. All life is sacred, and must be treated as such, if it was, then the turmoil that we see upon the Earth at present would cease, and the Earth would become what it was always intended to be, - another form of God's Heaven, one would not have to wait as it were, until one is released from the Earth-plane to seek what it is that we know as the "Kingdom of Heaven," for it should already dwell within the body that we inhabit whilst on Earth!

Live a simple but honest life with all of your fellow creatures that then, is the only truth that you need to seek. Truth is not as illusive as you seem to think it is. Just live for one another, and not against one another. You have been given many examples of how this can be done, even today you have living examples of that truth and yet do you learn the lesson that is shown to you? We say No, you turn a blind eye to what is obvious and go your own selfish way! Learn to accept your fellow man as another human being who is just like you, do not judge another one for actions which may seem to you to be different from yours. We are all the same and yet we are different in outlook but that should not be an obstacle to friendship and understanding. Life is too short, to squander even one day in thoughtlessness of another's plight. We all depend upon each other if we did but know it, but so often that simple teaching is ignored, and so you see all the disharmony that affects your world today. You cannot put off any longer the knowledge that tells you that your neighbour is in reality your very brother. Learn to live -and yes, let live. There is room upon your Earthplane for all of God's creatures to live harmoniously and not to cultivate hatred and envy of what another nation may have! And that also applies to individuals.' Love and understanding is not being weak, but it is in fact the strength that is lacking

26

in present day humanity. Turn back to God, for He is our Father and no other, learn to trust in Him, and in doing so you learn to trust your fellow man. It really is as simple as that, if only you can accept that truth, greed and envy are the stumbling blocks to a life of harmony, and where do they get you? Certainly not a peaceful existence if you look around you. Fear is what seems to be the norm these days and that only generates even more fear until it obscures what should be apparent to one and all, that envy of another's possessions can only lead to unhappiness for all concerned! Your world is in a turmoil and all because of envy and hatred, learn to give, not only goods but love and understanding to those in need, and then you will begin to see a world fit for all to live in, and yes- live in peacefully. It can be accomplished, but it needs strength in the purpose of sharing with one another and that does not mean only technology, but also understanding of anothers way of life. We cannot all be the same but our differences needn't mean that we have to dislike each other, for basically you will find many similarities that lie just beneath the surface, they only need to be aired and then you will find that you no longer hate what you do not understand! Your world can be a beautiful world to live in, and not one that is beset by fear, Show understanding to one another, they may not believe in what you do but who is to say that you are the only right way in that belief? Compromise is the answer, live and let live is the way forward, it is as simple as that, why not try the middle way instead of insisting that yours is the only right way and the other persons is the wrong one! Love is the Truth that is staring you in the face, accept the principle of that and you will find that life will begin to be what it was intended to be, one of peace and happiness and no longer one of fear and hatred. Learn to love yourselves, and then you will learn to love one another-with No reservations!

Chapter 11

When you leave this physical shell behind, and embark upon your new life in the Spirit World- what happens to you? What is "it" that leaves this mortal body for good? If you were to view that body after you have left it, -and many people do before they venture forth into what would seem to be the unknown, what would you perceive? Let us say that your transition has been peaceful, you now stand outside of that body that once was yours, what do you see? Do you look like the person that you have always imagined yourself to be? or is it a stranger lying there? One who seems familiar but is not quite what you thought of as "you"! For within the mortal body has dwelt for a lifetime one who has thought of itself as "ageless". That is how you felt, but the body that you now see before you is old, lined, and wrinkled, not even the shape that you remember you used to be? So who is "it" that is doing this viewing? This part of you that is very much alive and aware of it's surroundings? Could anyone who might be present be able to see this other you? We know that those with clairvoyant sight are able to, and what would they see, if asked? They would describe you as the same as the one upon the bed. A replica as it were! But would that one really be the "you" that we have been talking about? That spirit form is the cloak that houses that real essence of you that has left the physical body behind and is now ready to resume it's journey back to it's homeland, the World we all call 'Spirit'! Well now what does "it" do? Does it float away? Does it wait patiently for someone to come and give it directions? Or does it just stay and hope for the best? Well the answer to that is, in most cases, especially those who have a pretty good idea about the so-called Afterlife, for want of a better description, a light form of angelic appearance, together with some of those nearest and dearest to you, who have passed along this path before, are there to "escort" you to your next abode! You will be encased as it were in a warm vaporous substance, and you will still be surrounded by your loved ones, and without being aware of it you will find yourself once more, upon what you believe-as terra firma! You look around you, all seems familiar and yet you are sure you haven't been there before, but this does not worry you for you feel 'at home'. You experience a wonderful sense of peace and love, and so you drift as it were into a deep trance-like sleep. When you awake you have no idea how long you have rested, it could be minutes, days, months even, for time for you, has "stood still". You are now refreshed and ready for what awaits you! Your new life- span upon this your new world. There is much that intrigues you, for the light, and colours that surround you are of a luminosity and brightness that you have never beheld before, and yet to your eyes nothing is harsh, you just accept as natural whatever it is that you see and touch and experience. "Life force" seems to float around you, everything is effortless. You still have some of your loved ones with you for that is part of their desired duty to assist you in your adjusting to this new lifestyle! They have all gone through the same experience and so they know just what to do, and it is done with tenderness and love. You will now be taken to a very large building that has many, many rooms in it. You will be escorted to one of these rooms, and here your loved ones will leave you for a while, they do not enter with you. But you do have a guide and helper who will look after you. You enter what seems a room that is in shadow, but your eyes get accustomed to the gloom and you are able to see certain objects that are in the room, one is a chair or seat, upon which you are told you may sit, it is quite comfortable but it is not one that encourages you to slouch in it!

You are aware that there is some form of activity going on around you. You are told, though not in words but in thought that it is now time for you to review your past Earth life style and what it has taught you. You probably feel a little apprehensive and wonder just what it is that is to take place. In front of you, you are aware of what seems like a vaporous light, this gradually builds up into a circle that is not only in the round but is three dimensional. It forms a picture, a living picture that takes you back to the beginning of your life upon Earth. You witness your birth and the subsequent years that succeed it! Now you become aware of the "You" that you easily recognise. And now starts your reviewing in earnest! You see the whole of your life laid bare as it were, there are episodes that please you, and those that make you feel ashamed. You can as it were project yourself into this panoramic view and so understand not only your own feelings but those with whom you have been in contact, and how it has not only affected you but others also. This experience is shall we say, somewhat traumatic, but it is necessary if you are to start your new life with shall we say a "clean slate". Without realising it -you come to the end. The vapour disperses, and a soft light invades the room, you are told that you will be left alone for a while. There is soft music and the air is slightly perfumed. You suddenly realise that you have drifted into a sleep, for you are gently awakened with the words "well done, well done, you have purged yourself" "your friends await you". You find yourself outside of the room, and your loved ones embrace you and say"welcome home". This now is the start of your new and fruitful life. From hereon you are now responsible for all of your actions. You are about to embark upon a life of activity and understanding and of course, learning. There is so much for you to accomplish, you will in due course be shown various projects that are available to you to pursue, this will take the form of "classroom learning", not exactly a classroom in the Earthly sense, for this classroom is Life itself! You now find yourself with like-minded folk, some you know, others yet to be known, but you are all bound by the same desire for service to others. We have now brought you up to date as it were. The rest of your sojourn upon this Planet of Spirit growth is up to you. In another discourse we will tell you of the other spheres upon this Planet, for though you are all spirit form you never the less are not all of the same race or culture! Or for that matter speech! That will make you think, for you thought that being Spirit will automatically enable you to converse with all and sundry! You can, but it takes time and effort-and more importantly Thought.

Chapter 12

It is truth that you seek dear Brother, and the truth is all around you, but it is difficult to perceive it. For there are so many variations of what is termed upon the Earthplane as a Truth! Truth comes from within, it is the inner knowledge that is imparted to you from the self that is known as Spirit! That part of you that has the ability to collect the knowledge of the ancients and impart to those of today who have ears to hear with, and eyes to see with, and here we do not speak of the organs of the physical body in which your Spirit dwells!

Truths have always been available to those who seek them with an open mind and a heart that is in unison with the God given breath of Life! In other words- Listen, learn and then put into practice what it is that you feel you have been told! There is only one truth and yet it has many variations that are yet still fundamentally the same basic Truth! That no doubt strikes you as not only confusing but also a negation of what is said! For to behold the truth in all it's glory is given to but very few and those who are vouch-saved this privilege have been weighed as it were and found to be worthy of being initiated into those hidden truths, and what are these hidden truths?? -that man is forever seeking?

The riddle of the Universe and all that lies within it's boundaries, and what the life of those who dwell upon it's many so-called Worlds of experience is capable of, and why! The riddle of life is life itself! It takes more than one lifetime to come to that conclusion! And when one has, what is it that man does with this Divine knowledge? He hoards it to himself as if it is gold, and does not dare to share it with others! But truth when found must be shared, and not kept to oneself, otherwise that truth becomes obsolete and is now no longer seen as a truth!

[The whole of life is forever changing, today you are not the same as yesterday, and tomorrow you will be different from today] And yet you will not notice the difference but never the less it is a truth that we give to you, if you stop and think about it! You cannot stand still and think that you have progressed! For to remain stationary means that for you, life has ceased to be life! Think about it carefully! You must be forever changing, not only your bodily tissues but also your mental outlook! Nothing stands still in God's World it is forever on-going, being re-born, and yet remaining as it were the same! For God is unchangeable and yet is forever changing! - and how is that? It is in man's perception of Him! If you are living the life that you should, then each day you will perceive just a little bit more of what God is all about! Never the full conception, for that has to be earned and learned the hard way! And that way is the way of all flesh! Until you are able to dispense with that outer covering and emerge into the light of greater understanding! That only comes about when your journey's upon the realm of Earth have ceased and you are reborn once again into your Spirit body of realisation of who you are! And does it end there? Why No! tis just the beginning of a new round of living experiences that are to take you further up the ladder of progress The Ladder, is another name for Mind! For it is with the Mind that one learns how to fulfil what it is that has been ordained from the very beginning of time itself!

The truth that one seeks is the truth that we are part of the Creator of all Truth, and as such we must accept that responsibility, for to be the explainers of truth is a great privilege and yes - a great responsibility, for if we are to be the purveyors of God's Truths then we must be prepared to be open, to not only injustice but even ridicule by those who abhor the truth, for they prefer to remain in ignorance and pursue their own corrupt way of life, until one day they realise that they can no longer hide from it!

And yet the truth is really so simple and straight forward. It is just living a God Like Life, in all it's aspects! But to many people that seems an impossibility. But is it? Not really, it just means putting self not first but last! In other words, trying to understand the other person or Nation! For nations are made up of people are they not? When people change, then the nations will cease their envy of each other and learn to live in peace and harmony. Then you will see truth as it is meant to be seen. Love one another in the true Universal sense, then all those facets of the Truth, will merge as one glorious one! And that is God. Know your God, and that is knowing yourself as part of Him, know Him as your Brother, your Mother, your Sister and yes- your Father! We are all part of the fabric of The Almighty. That is The Truth. Live by that precept, and one day you will not only understand what is the Truth, you will be that Truth made manifest! Search no more dear friends. The Truth abides within you and always has been. Release it and know that Truth is GOD!

Chapter 13

Mankind has always wondered just what is the reason for his journey which he believes starts upon this plane of existence known to you as Earth! He feels that this can only be a beginning, but a beginning to what? The reason eludes him, for to most of mankind the proof of a future existence beyond this realm has never really satisfied that part of him that he knows is not just the part he uses and knows as himself. Yet to delve too deeply into the subconscious for an answer has been taboo for many, other than those who have been brought up in that form of so-called religious culture, where communion with the so-called Dead has been a part of his life that has long remained a mystery and one that he has tampered with in a form of wanting an explanation that would only satisfy his curiosity and that is all. He has not really wanted to look deeper for if he had he would know that it is up to him to satisfy this thirst for knowledge, and that would involve altering his whole lifestyle, and this he has not been prepared to do, and so he just tampers with what is commonly known as the occult and hoped that he would receive answers to his mundane thoughts of what life has to offer him, and not what he has to offer to life!

It is, a two way offering this questioning, for once man has opened up his inner senses then there is no turning back, he is then on the road of discovering his true identity and that means a complete re-adjusting of all his preconceptions of what this and the other lives are all about. This one is just one of many, and if you tell the majority of mankind that this body of his is but one of many that he will have to inhabit on this journey back to the source of his very creation, he will scoff at the suggestion and turn away, because he does not want to know that he is responsible for his very life's work, he prefers to think that things happen to him that he is not ultimately responsible for. He is a coward for it is Himself that is responsible for all of his actions and he cannot shirk that responsibility. Once he accepts that, then he has begun to live in real earnest.

His other self can then take over and guide him in his every day activities and by his "other self" we are talking of that one that you term 'Spirit', which is the real one that dwells within the outward shell called man. Though here we must try and explain what we all think of at one time as 'Spirit'. You call the "other world"(another misnomer) Spirit, because you have no other word to justify it's existence, you think that it is some form of illusive place that one perhaps gravitates to when death encompasses the mortal body. But it is the so-called Spirit that lives and never dies, for it does not need to when it is time for it to readjust itself to it's new surroundings. People think of this other side of man as an illusive type of nonmaterialistic being, when it is really the only real one that he is! This mortal body is merely a cloak of identity suitable for this planet of yours but is not the real person, that is there but unseen not only by others but more often than not! not even by the one who is the cloak of protection. Think upon that. We all need some form of what has been termed "reference" in other words a seeing, living, breathing,form that can be recognised as a human form! When you transfer to the world that you call spirit, you are free from that restrictive vehicle you have been using, and so take on another one less dense and more malleable in every way, one that is suitable to the world that you now inhabit. This is your Real World, and yet this is only one of the many that you will in turn dwell upon in your upward progression.

Once you have discarded the physical body, you are now free of that encumbrance, and can really learn what you are truly made up of. That is The Life Force from the source of all Creativity. We are but a form of that Creativity for there are many, many forms that stem from that source, "Man" is but one of them. He it is that is the only one that can claim to be in the likeness of what he calls the Creator. But is he? Will he ever know? That is one of the reasons for his being alive in the first place. WE, and we stress that word, we are all part of His Creation, and though we are told we are in His likeness, that is only to try and give mankind a form of reference to go by. For we could never be like the Creator if you care to think about it in those terms! The Creator of All cannot possibly be a like creature that man can identify himself with can he? And yet he is part of this creative principle and so must have some of those attributes mustn't he? So why doesn't he try to be more like this one that he loosely terms God?! If he did start to behave like he should, then all this turmoil that he finds himself in would take on a completely different aspect. He would see what it is all for and how he must not only adapt to it, but also overcome it in other words Live. Preparing himself for the upward journey that he must eventually take if he is to reach the goal that has been set for him to achieve!

Earth is but a ground of preparation, learning, and not only overcoming but growing in stature, and that does not mean physically, but here we use that term again, Spiritually! So that when he re-emerges back to that body of his that is his "real" self he will be better equipped to deal with this new existence that is just a small part of his overall lifestyle that has been planned for him!

So you see it really is Man's own responsibility to fit himself for these coming lives, he cannot expect someone to do it for him. However much he would like to pass on the responsibility for his own actions! Start to accept that you are your own Master, and not a servant, you must take on this responsibility for your own actions and how they affect those around you. Whatever we do affects others as well as ourselves, so try and see that the effect is beneficial to all concerned, and not just to oneself! That way we grow, and not only this outward body, but the one within, the one that knows who it is, and why it is!

Look upon this physical vehicle as a necessary piece of apparatus, that has been loaned to you while you are upon this plane of learning, accept it for what it is, a temporary home for the Living Spirit within. The real one, not the illusory one that you see in the mirror when you awake in the morning. There's far more to you than that reflection, that you see! Look within, get used to the real you, learn to live with yourself, accept that there is more to you than you realise. Open up your mind to the possibilities of who you are and what you can achieve, then and only then will you really come alive!

Chapter 14

You have been told recently about what it is you -and that does mean mankind in general will do when once you have adjusted to your new way of life upon the next sphere in your round of evolutionary progress. Well of course there is so much more to this life than what we have been able to convey to you via these pages! Life is far more complex, than shall we say a set of rules to go by and leave it at that. You see little friend, we do not change our way of thinking or even or attitudes just because we have cast aside the mortal body and taken upon ourselves the one of the Spirit!

You will argue that as it is the Spirit body -and that means the person within it, we should be in possession of much higher thinking and doing than when we were upon the Earthplane. Well in theory that is correct but remember we are all human, and that goes for the Spirit entity as well, and just because we spend some of our secret life upon the Spirit World while still dwelling within the physical body, does not automatically endow us with extra-terrestrial abilities! You see dear friends, this next world in your journey ever upwards is only a stones throw away from your earth-bound one, and so as it overlaps and is part of that one, it naturally has a lot of the same attributes and is not quite what many souls think it is going to be!

You have toiled all of your lives and that leaves upon you a scar that has to be cleaned away, leaving shall we say healthy tissue! This is all metaphorical! In other words the life that you have led has given you certain thoughts, desires, and outlooks, that need to be tempered -and in some cases obliterated all together before you can start to re-adjust to your new and permanent surroundings. This is your New Life! Your new round of experiences and thoughts that are to carry you forward in your next round on the evolutionary scale! So you can see dear friends that there is quite a lot of re-adjusting, re-learning to be done before you can even contemplate beginning to learn to live here upon this plane, and when we say live we mean just that! For living here is one of not only joy but also of being aware of how what you do, think, or are, affects all of those around you! This does not come about overnight so to speak, It takes work and that means hard work mentally to cast off all those old inhibitions and start afresh! We understand for we have had to travel the same path and so we are patient as well as being helpful to each new soul that awakens to this new lifestyle! You see what we are getting at? You do not change for shall we say "the better" just by the mere fact that you have exchanged one mode of living for another! Adjustment is what it is all about. That is, your whole mental attitude! For it is that part of you that is indestructible and goes on and on, regardless of what body you are going to inhabit. Even your Spirit body has been affected shall we say, by the outlook of the physical and so it too needs to re-adjust itself to the new existence even though it has been inhabiting the Spirit

World "on and off" all through the physical bodies lifetimes! People tend to think that as Spirit you must be all knowing, all seeing, all understanding, but that takes "time", you do not automatically cast aside a life-times thinking and acting just because you now dwell upon the starry heights you call Spirit Land! Your whole lifetime upon Earth was to prepare you for your next lifetime upon the realm of Spirit, and so you have learned how to live! Or should we say that is what was expected of you when you incarnated upon that Planet! We so often fall short of the goals that our Spirit sets for us, before embarking upon this lower sphere! But then that is the reason for being here, to learn how to overcome what life throws at you, that is what is called 'the art of living'! You cannot hope to accomplish this in one brief lifespan upon Earth, hence the need to reincarnate time and time again until such time as your Spirit self knows that you are ready to quit the wheel of lives upon Earth, and begin the next round here in the Spirit World of high existence, where you start to live all over again, but this time with inner knowledge of what is expected of you! Your life upon the Spirit plane of existence will be one not only of high expectancy but one of learning the joy of being really alive! And that means the "mind substance" that governs all activity whether upon Earth or Elsewhere! Think about that, for that organ is your lifeline to Eternity. The thread that sustains you and links you with the One who is the Creator of all life forms! The Soul that awaits you upon one of the many Higher spheres is the last link in the chain, and when you reach that plane of existence, then you really have learnt the lessons that were prepared for you before you even existed!

Never despise yourself when you fall short of your expectations either upon the Earthplane or when you are here on our side of life. You are born to learn and you cannot learn if you do not make mistakes. That is the only way to cope with all the complexities of living and that goes just as much for your life upon the Spirit realm as for your sojourn upon the lower realm called Earth. So you see dear friends, progress is a somewhat slow process is it not? To win our way back to the source of all Creation takes what you know as "time". Time, though an illusion is also a reality when it is needed in the evolutionary scale of progress! To dispense with time is not necessarily an advantage all the 'time'. Think upon that one! For to be timeless means that you have achieved oneness, and to achieve oneness means a lifetime's work, and that encompasses many so-called lifetimes upon many, many spheres! As you can see, life is not just cut and dried, it is a form of learning how to live to one's capacity, for we all have far more than we realise. Once upon this sphere, you begin to see how you can really use all of your "potentials". This sphere shows you "how", the next sphere shows you "why" and the next? Well we will leave that for the present, for you have a long way to go before you reach even that one! And when you do, then you too will look back and see where you have come from, and see others who need the hand of help that we are extending to you dear friends upon the Earth.

Chapter 15

It has crossed your mind regarding these inhabitants that dwell upon the distant planets, you wonder if they really do exist and if so what sort of relationship do they have with the people of the Earth. They are your Brothers! What you might term your Elder Brethren! No, not in years but in psychic understanding, they have knowledge and attributes far in advance of yours, but they wish to help you in your evolution! They understand about your lack of progress not only in the field of the mind but also of the psychic! They have, as it were perfected this union of body and Spirit, not only knowing of it's existence in the so-called Spirit realm but also having the ability to "switch" from one to the other when it is required! One day, but not for a very long time in your scale of time you too will have this ability, but sadly not for the foreseeable future for you have much to learn about yourselves before that comes about! Here we are talking not only of your "Spirit" self but of those others that dwell upon another sphere of existence, waiting for you to -shall we say "catch up" with them! Yes dear friends they or rather "you" are alive and living another form of life, not as yet known to your lower bodies of existence! But that is all we are allowed to say on that particular subject. We will now continue with those other beings that we have called your 'elder Brothers'. They dwell upon planets far distant from yours and yet they are of a similar structure and here we are talking of the planet as well as the inhabitants! They understand this structure of yours and can live shall we say upon your Earthplane without any form of discomfort to the body that they are inhabiting while sojourning on your planet! By which you may gather that some of 'them' are already living amongst you! Many of your 'thinking' brethren have an inkling of this but hesitate to broadcast the fact for fear of being labelled cranks to put it mildly. But believe us they do dwell amongst you, and they 'come and go' at will! They do not need your so-called flying saucers to do this form of travelling! They have the ability to transfer one body to another, lowering or highering their vibrations according to circumstances. You see they are shall we say human as well as Spirit all at the same time, but unlike you upon the Earth, they live in both worlds simultaneously! Perhaps this is difficult for you to understand but it is true, we have that ability as well for we too travel back and forth to other spheres when necessary!

The planets or Earths or whatever you like to call them can and do exchange not only inhabitants, but shall we say Technology as well. This is quite an ordinary occurrence among the planets that are in communication with each other. That is one of the reasons why those volunteers for they are volunteers come to your Earth to monitor your life-force and life style.

They study you very very carefully and then 'report' back to their homeland via "our Spirit World" That must surprise you! You see, we are all one really, even though our spheres and vibrations may differ we are all part of this overall plan of on-going evolutionary life all over the Universe! And beyond! Those 'volunteers' that we speak of will one day be not only a part of your Earth vibrations but they will be the fore runners of those who are to inhabit your Earth plane in the far off distant future! Your 'species' as you have been told before is to be 'upgraded', They will have unlocked the knowledge that they have inherited and so will be of a higher form of human life, those who will replace you are ready to make of this Earth a less dense form of existence both within and without! For by then the inner life will have become a complimentary life style,if you can follow what we are saying! You are being monitored and evaluated so that those who are to follow you will have acclimatised themselves to the lower plane which is to be their plane of "learning" as it is yours now! In time you upon Earth will have left this sphere for one that is "higher up the scale". That is those who warrant that transformation, those who don't will be absorbed into the then living organisms, so that they can in time progress as it has been ordained!

So much that will happen in the future, or rather is happening in the Now for change is ever on-going, it never stops! This world of yours and ours is not static, it is forever growing and learning and adapting, that is progress and that is what living a life is all about! Those Brothers that we spoke of are to help you in this progress. Gradually they will be able to influence those who are in what you term "authority" and so this gradual enlightenment will become normality and so the progress though gradual will be permanent and in a way not noticed by the population! Such is progress! It is always happening but not always understood as such! All "worlds" and we use that term loosely are dependent upon each other even when they are independent, or so it would seem! We are all learning gradually about each other so that in time we live in Harmony with each other, exchanging ideas and yes even populations if so desired! Space is not a reality it is an illusion of the here and now! One day it will all come together and time will then be of no importance, there will be no "past tense" for the past and the future will be the Now! A lot for you to get your "teeth into" dear friends of the Earth but you will, you will, That is why we are here to try and enlighten you to prepare you, though in actual fact these happenings will not affect you upon the Earth-plane at this stage!

Chapter 16

Think! And what are your thoughts? You have toyed with the idea of Distant lands of the World known as Spirit! And you have wondered what they may be like and if they really do exist outside of your own imagination! Cease your wondering Brother, they are real, and they do exist! Your World that is known to you as Earth, is not the only World of human habitation. All other worlds or planets of habitation are realities! They are Not figments of someone's imagination. Just because they cannot be observed or identified does not mean that they do not exist! Our World is basically the same as yours land masses, mountains, seas, continents, in fact they could almost be said to mirror your own World, we too have "areas" that are somewhat unknown to us! Strange as that may seem to you, it is nevertheless true! We too have our "explorers" those who wish to venture into the unknown parts of our Universe! There is much that is till not understood about this World, that is your companion! You see dear friend life does exist and exists to be explored! And that need not mean quite what it seems! For "life", though understood by many as being lived can also refer to the "inner" world of the individual! Yes! Dear friend, even so-called Spirit people have inner worlds of existence. Just because we inhabit this next sphere that adjoins yours, does not mean that it is completely known to it's inhabitants! There are "areas" or we should say Continents that have remained in a state of virgin territory, unexplained and unexplored! Which brings us to the next phase in this discussion about the World of the Spirit! We and in time you will understand that life upon this sphere is one of exploration not only of places but of oneself! Yes, of oneself! For you do have Experiences here that are unfamiliar to you, we say "to you" and we mean that that includes us as well! We are learning all the time just as we did when dwelling upon the Earth, and you learn by "doing" and that means coping with what might be termed the "unexpected"! If there were no areas, and that includes man himself, that were unknown there would be no incentive to find out what this and other lives have to offer! Do you see where we are leading you to? Life here is very much an on-going experience in every way. Just because you have left the Earth body behind it does not mean that you are not to live a full life "over here"! and a "full life" means one of learning and coping, situations will arise that will need your ability to overcome them and profit from the experience! You will be in a position to evaluate any situation that may arise even sometimes before it materialises! That is when you have learnt how to! You see, you are still learning about life and how it affects you, it hasn't suddenly stopped being a challenge for that is what living is all about is it not? A challenge is something that stimulates you, makes you think and then act accordingly! Now do you see what we are getting at? Your life has not ceased, you do not sit around doing nothing in particular! That would not be Heaven if

40

that is what you think this next phase is! For as we have told you before, This is not the Heaven of your story books! It is a World of Action! And that does not mean turmoil, it merely means that you learn to use your mental powers as they should be used. You had to, while you tarried upon Earth didn't you? Well it is no different here!

Now, that brings us back to the start of this discourse! Lands Continents and suchlike, that may be termed 'foreign' if you like! And that also goes for those who inhabit them! Being a Spirit does not mean that you are all alike, far from it! How dull and uninspiring that would be, don't you agree? It is the variability of not only persons but locations that stimulate a thinking person, and believe us , thought here is for Thinking and Learning and that means learning how to use that capacity as it was intended to be used! Thought is the productive part of any person who uses their Intelligence, in the art of being alive. For to live is to progress and to progress is to live! You will encounter all sorts of shall we say, unknown forms of living matter upon this World of the Spirit! For here thought becomes a living reality in whatsoever capacity it is being used. Do you follow? Reality is only real when you make it so! And when you understand what true reality is! By which we mean that illusion of one sort or another plays a very big part in everyday learning! Illusion can be real when required! Paradox! Yes, but true! You learn to differentiate the different forms of illusion and reality. For not all reality need be what it seems!

So you see dear friends you are in for quite a shock if you were under the delusion that everything on the Spirit World was what you had been led to think of as ordered and therefore not to be wondered at! Expect the unexpected and then you will begin to understand what living on this sphere of learning is all about! Do not be daunted by what we have said to you, you quickly learn how to adapt to your new life once you are here. It is full of surprises and let us hasten to add-of the nicest kind! You are here to progress towards your next goal, it does not come easily, it requires effort on your part, but then the "rewards" for the effort made are truly worth it as you will soon see!

So you can look forward to a fulfilling life-cycle if you wish it! It is entirely up to you. Learn to live and accept and you will find that you really are living now as you have never lived before! Look forward to your new life, explore it, enjoy it for there is so much for you to do with your new found freedom, freedom of thought and activity! Remember that here thought becomes reality when thought is properly used! And that does require thought, think upon that!

In another discourse we will delve deeper into those unknown areas that we hinted at in the beginning. Areas that will inspire and excite you and stimulate your thought process. There is so much here for you to marvel at, for here "Creation" can become a reality! We leave you on that note.

Chapter 17

When we say "God Bless You" what is it that we mean? It is not just those words. For it is what lies beyond and then that is the important thing. Words are spoken to convey what the speaker is not only thinking but what it is that they wish to convey and what is a "Reality". Not the abstract thought but a substance that is not only real but is alive and meaningful, a "Reality" in every sense of that word. And what is that Reality? It is the Union with the almighty that we are talking about. A union of real substance and not just in the mind. But of course that is where it is started from and from that thought it matures into a real and living vibration, a "Union" in every sense of the word. To "Bless" what does that one word signify? When you say that to another person it so often is just a phrase. "God Bless You" a lovely expression, but the sentiment goes deeper than the words that are being expressed. To bless someone is a form of trying to give to them what it is that God has given to us! His Blessing is His Love and that means not just a word but something that is real and tangible and so when we say to another being "Bless You" we are actually giving to them God's Love that he has bestowed upon us, to give and to use in His Name. They are not meant to be just an idle expression. When you say "Bless You" it should be given from the very heart and soul of that person to whoever you are wishing to convey that feeling. It is in actual fact A Union with God! And so you are joining together not only yourself but our own Father God Creator and that union brings those two souls into contact with their Creator, 3 in 1! That trio of love that will conquer all things. So when you next utter those three words, think, think what do they and you mean. You are asking God to give to that person not just a word but a real and living substance. Love, a word that is used too often but what is the meaning behind that utterance? When you say Love you are actually giving up part of yourself to another being just as God has given you Life through his Love for you, you are in turn saying to that other person "here take part of my life, I give it to you freely". That is what Love really is, a giving, a sharing of your own life substance. A joining together.

So when you now in the future say to another person God Bless You, really mean it, and in saying those three words you are actually asking God to embrace that person with His and your love. For when you truly mean what you say then you are actually being part of what that word Love is all about. We have been given that capacity to give to one another in an outward as well as an inward expression of God's bounteous love in His creation of a being in His own likeness! When we learn to begin to give to others what has been given to us, then we are really living a God Life which translated is a Good Life in every aspect. If we can truly live that form of existence then we are really beginning to Live as we should. Gone will be the envy, the jealousy, the hurtful word, and in their place will blossom a flower of beauty, of compassion, in other words of Love!

What a wonderful world this could be if we live by that principle. No more war and no more hatred, for Love would erase all those things. They cannot thrive when Love is expressed, and that means from the Heart and not just from the Voice. We urge you to start now. Look within yourself, know just who you are and what you are. You are part of the Almighty as He is part of you. That inner part that is always striving to make itself felt to the outward one that you call You! We are more than just this outward covering we call a body. We are a spirit, a soul, an essence of the divinity. That is what we are, part of the divine, we are not separate from it, we are a living part of that Divinity, so learn to live like one! You are God's in the making. You have that potential. It has been given to you and given to you freely! Learn to give it to others and you will find that life will become a thing of beauty. For when it starts from within it manifests without and you will become in truth a Son of God and then you can behave as one and give to your brothers God's Love which is this very blessing made manifest.

Look in your mirror each day to see beyond the reflection that looks back at you. Look deeper and see the God person what dwells therein and start the day with the words "I do love what I am" and really mean it and Live it. Make each day a Union with God and in that way you are leading a life of fulfilment. Love your neighbour as yourself. It really does work. And each day the bond grows ever stronger, you are working for God and He is working through you.

Chapter 18

When Jesus was upon the earth in mortal flesh form, life was very different from today. People were expecting a redeemer. One who would change their lives for ever! But dear friends, people are their own redeemer if they could but see it! We all look for one that is without and yet the redeeming starts from within and that is where you have to look to find the One you would call your Redeemer. The Christ Spirit! That is what the act of redemption is all about. We are all one with that Eternal Spirit if we can only accept that fact and cease trying to find one that will appear to us in a mortal form and so show us the way to go that will take us back to the home that we left so long ago! Christ or Jesus the man, was a forerunner of what mankind could become if he only trusted in his own inner source of Christ consciousness! For the consciousness of Christ is within each and every one, regardless of their ethnic origin, creed or culture. And yes even the colour of their outward skin of protection. Christ that is the consciousness is shall we say Colour Blind! And that is how we all should be. Colour is just a different form of pigmentation of the skin. Below the surface we are all the same! And that is how we should acknowledge each other, as Brothers in that consciousness. Yes Brothers and not strangers. For a stranger is only a person who you have not yet known! Look beneath the surface and there is no longer what you thought was a stranger, but a fellow creature, begat by the One on High as an emissary of His Love. Learn to see and feel that love for one and other and all your differences will fade away. When you look in the mirror try and visualise yourself as if you were another person. Look hard and see that the one whose reflection stares back at you is more than just that face that you recognise and call Me!

Christ as he was known was and is the true brother of one and all, in fact all of mankind! He may be called by many names and even take on the appearance of another race but He is the Christ Consciousness, the one aspect that God Almighty has shown his face to his creatures of his own creation. Do you not yet understand that God is Christ and Christ is God and that means that we are All a part of that great Divinity! So why do we think that another soul is a stranger? He is indeed your other self, your twin soul if you like. So treat that one as you would treat the brother of your own family. For we are all part of the family of our Father in Heaven are we not?! Begin to live as Brothers. Do not turn your back upon your neighbour, for who knows he could be your next kith and kin if you did but know it. And here we refer to your next journey upon the planet you call Earth! For believe us dear friend, reincarnation is a Fact of Life. It has to be, for how can we hope to become what we know we should be in the span of our lifetime upon this planet of the lower spheres?!

You are born to live for eternity. No not as a human like body, but one of Spirit Essence which takes upon itself these outward forms of expression so that others may identify with each other until the time comes when Spirit knows itself as Spirit and no longer needs a physical garment to express its identity! As we progress upon the pathway of our many lives of existence, we change, we change all the time without actually being aware of this change and so we no longer require this outward form of reference. We become part of each other and yet we still remain our own identity. We have altered our perception of who and what we are. We begin to see that we are all part of each other and that is the Mind Perception. For that is how we change our attitude to our outward appearance. We no longer look without but "see" to "be" the inner being of light that we freely are!

Light is but a refraction of an unseen quantity that exists but is not always apparent to the naked eye! In other words we are but we are Not! Difficult for you to grasp perhaps, but it is nevertheless a fact and a truth! We are, shall we say, a substance that is "fluid" if that is the right explanation! We reflect what and where we are for we are that very substance that makes us who we are, whether seen or unseen makes no difference. We just Are and that means in layman's terms we are part of the living God of all Creation! We must all come to that realisation sometime. There is no getting away from it and when we finally realise just who we really are and where we originate from, then our journeys through life will cease to matter for we are back to this source of All Life. But dear friends be not daunted for that time shall we say is not only in the future, but is part of eternity and eternity goes on forever does it not! We return to our beginning. We all have the spirit of Christ consciousness within us. Awaken that spirit and learn to live as Spirit in Human Form. Be a reflection of the one who once walked upon this earth of yours, who was and is like You. But He knew who he was and lived accordingly and yes still does. For the Christ Spirit or consciousness is eternal and can never die, has always been and always will be! And that dear friend means you and I in fact all of us.

Become the God that you are for in truth we come from God then we must be God mustn't we? Or shall I say a Reflection of God. Like the reflection in a pool of clear water, ripple it with your hands and the reflection alters. But when the water is still once more the reflection is the same. We alter and yet we return as we were originally. So that is how we go back to our source of creation. Look in the pool once more and as you see your own reflection do you not see the one that is the pool? The one behind the one who is looking? God the Creator is that pool. He is everywhere and in everything. That is our Life to know who and what we not only are but who

45

we are to one day become! Christ was the manifested form of the one who is Unknowable. See him in all that you do and are for he is truly your Brother in the consciousness of the Holy Spirit Jesus the man and Christ His Spirit just as you are! Man and spirit. Spirit and man. All one. Live in that knowledge and live by that knowledge and you will find that life is truly worth the living however hard it may seem at times. Look for the spirit within and learn to live with that spirit so that in reality your spirit is seen from without by others and not hidden away as is so often the case for fear of being, shall we say, misunderstood? Do not, as the scriptures say, "Hide your light under a bushel". Let it be seen by one and all as a reflection of the One upon High and you will be amazed at the difference life will become and not only for you dear friends but for others as well!

Chapter 19

Once in a while you may come across in a book or an article in a paper or magazine something that makes you sit up and take notice of what you have read. You may even go back and read it over and over again. Your mind has been stimulated with fresh thoughts. You perhaps have been given a fresh perspective on an old question or one that has been pushed far back into your subconscious without you realising it. That is what we aim to do. Not just to you dear friend but to those others of like minds.

Such a lot of misinformation has been promulgated over the centuries regarding not only this life (the one of the Earthplane) but also of the life to come! People have such vague ideas as to what life is really all about and what it is ultimately for! You are told that you reincarnate upon the lower sphere called Earth to help you to discover who you are and why you are as you are! But are you really any the wiser? Sadly not often for you feel perhaps confused. One tells you one thing and then another tells you something quite different. And like the old saying "Between two stools you fall to the ground!" Your life is your life and no one else's. So what is said or read must be pertinent to you and you only! In other words you have to come to a conclusion that will satisfy your curiosity and enlighten you into the bargain! Now where does that leave you? For in most cases you cannot possibly verify for yourself what you have been informed! And yet you have you know! For when one lifetime comes to its end and you are once more upon the realm of the spirit, you see for yourself what it is that has been bothering you while you were upon the Earthplane! So why you ask do you not remember these things if and when you return to the earth in another incarnation? Well dear friends you do! It is all in your so call Subconscious! Unfortunately we are not yet endowed with the ability to tap into this part of our life by ourselves! We seem to require an outside influence to do this for us and that influence which is usually a person who specialises in these things does not always delve in the right direction and you have to rely upon their interpretation of past events which Is not always accurate! One day we may be able to do this for ourselves when we are able to contact our other self, the one we call our subconscious which is a reality if we only knew it! It is an extension of the physical person. Perhaps we may say the real person who is always in the background, never able to come to the fore! If they were then the physical being would find coping with the real life much easier in every way! No preconceived notions, no inhibitions that clutter up the senses. For you would be able to make decisions that are correct and not perhaps flawed in their outcome! But that cannot yet come about, it will in due time, but not yet, not until we have "grown up" so to speak!

We are speaking dear friend of those upon the Earthplane and not those of us in the Spirit World! For we have no need of a subconscious. We are that Consciousness! In reality! That is to say those of us who dwell permanently upon the Realms of the Spirit! As you too will one day! We are still learning about the so called "mysteries of life". Which we are told are really not mysteries when you understand the underlying reasons behind what is termed a mystery and then it no longer is, for it has become a reality and a known one at that! Perhaps the mysteries are those other planets of existence that hover in the universe and beckon us to explore their lifestyles! In time planets or worlds or spheres, whatever name you wish to call them, will be more widely known about and seen and perhaps visited by others. Perhaps that is the final outcome of the plan of the One most High or should we have said One's most High! For there are others who are responsible for the outcome of those worlds as yet unknown to Man! But who are never the less shall we say our Brothers in the cycle of life or lives for they will one day be interchangeable! Yes that is a fact! The movement between the various spheres can and will be a reality! When harmony reigns amongst not only nations but the galaxies themselves! Now that is a mystery worth exploring is it not! But no! not yet a while! Earth man has a long way to go before he reaches those heights!

So you see dear friends upon the earth there is so much more to "life" than you can ever visualise in your present state of evolution! The universes, the cosmos, the sheer vastness of creation is beyond our meagre power of thought. We just are not programmed yet to be able to comprehend what the true meaning of life is really for, or all about! We must be content to accept that what has been decreed is for our benefit and when the time is right we shall know more and here we are speaking not of the foreseeable future for that span of life is so far off as not even to be thought of as a reality! Try and accept the limitations of our present understanding and that means each and everyone of us! Do not try to delve too deeply into what is unknowable at this present stage of man's evolution. Learn to live the simple life of goodness and understanding of other's lifestyles! They may not agree with what you think is correct, but it may be for them! If they are in a error, they will know it someday and then they too will come round to rethinking what their lives are all about. You cannot hurry progress either for nations or for individuals. Accept, reject and then accept again! That is what life is all about. There is No Mystery it is knowing and living how God in His Wisdom has shown us can be lived, living a life that is a benefit to all and not just for oneself!

You are your own judge. You are the master of your own thoughts and actions. See to it that you live to the best of your own ability and not how others think you should. Trust in God and your own intuition for it is god given if you did but know it!

48

Chapter 20

Dear Brethren of the Earth we speak to you of past events that not only have a bearing upon your present age but also give you an insight of what may in the future be your destiny! If we may start with the books that you call "Holy" and here we do not speak of just the Religion called "Christianity". For books or manuscripts of other faiths are also considered by them as Holy and are so reverenced because of their contents! But you must realise that those books and manuscripts were written for that day and age and though they can still have an influence on today's populations, they should Not always be taken literally! Or as some would say Gospel! And not to be tampered with or even questioned as to their meaning or authority! They were guidelines as it were for those in those far off times for living a righteous life, one of unselfish behaviour and tolerance of others beliefs! Sadly they no longer are seen or understood for the values that they promulgated! Tolerance of each other does not seem to weigh very much in today's society and if we are honest they were not practised very much even in the days when they were written and espoused! You, that is of the Christian faith, were given a prime example in the Christ Spirit of how Man can live and should live! But what did they do to the one who showed them the way? They tried and some would say successfully to stifle what was being said and taught by that Divine Teacher! But their success was short-lived wasn't it? For His teachings are very much alive today and will continue to be so! But! They must be read in the context that they were spoken by him. When they were written which was sometime after his departure from this life they were not always reported as He said or even meant them to be understood. Like most of the stories in that Holy Book they have to be not only read but analysed and their contents sifted and used in today's idiom! Which is entirely different from those far off days and events! So what we are saying is in today's vocabulary "read between the lines"! and do not accept everything you read as Gospel or written in Stone! Use your intelligence and see if what you read can be considered applicable for today's lifestyle! You'll find much that can be used for it is timeless in its original concept. Think upon that "in its original concept". Without all of the trimmings that seemed to have obscured what was being said and taught! And this goes for all of the Holy literature from all of the various so called Religions of this World!

If you really study them you will come to the conclusion that fundamentally they all express the same basic truths. Tolerance is what they are saying and if you really and sincerely practice that then these wars of yours would become things of the past! They promulgate because Man only gives "lip service" to what has been written in his holy scriptures but the reality of his actions belie the teachings that he pretends to abide by! Look back at history and even today. Religion has been the excuse for trampling upon another person's lifestyle"" You are hypocrites and an affront to the Almighty whatever name you wish to give Him! Religion has become a byword for Man's intolerance of others faiths or beliefs! You will never be able to force your beliefs upon another if they do not wish it! You may think you have to, probably because you think that God is not only on your side but has given you the authority in His name to coerce others to your way of thinking and acting! What gives you the right to use God's Name for your own actions that so often result in not only hatred of the one who professes his good intentions as if they have the blessings and permission of the One on High, but deep down they still believe what they want to believe. And who is to say that they are not right in doing so? Even your so called Religions cannot always see eye to eye with each other. Why on earth do you not learn to live and let live. Leave others alone. God is big enough to cope with all of the Religious beliefs. He doesn't need telling what you think are his desires on the subject of so called Religion! It's just Man's way of trying to curry favour with the Almighty and He is Not deceived believe me! Better no religion at all than the sham facade that Man calls his Religious calling! When you hear a person say God has called them! Look beneath the surface and you may be surprised at what you find!

We come back again and again to that word Tolerance, for that is what the teachings of those Masters of the past taught. It doesn't matter who they were or are they spoke this word of God and not of Man. Tolerance, understanding and love, 3 in one, one in 3! Live by those principles and you won't go far wrong in this your one of many lives yet to come.

We leave you with this Blessing of the One on High for all people everywhere. You are Brothers try and act like them and cease your bickering amongst yourselves for really it gets you nowhere in the long run does it?

Chapter 21

Life seems to rush past one and you wonder where it has gone to! When you are young the thought of the so called after life is the last thing that crosses your mind for you have plenty to occupy your thoughts just getting through each day. But there does come a time when you begin to wonder just what this life is all about and where is it getting you. Then all at once you realise that soon this life will come to an end and then what? Some people just think that that is it. Nothing more! Such a waste of thought if they think that all that has happened to them through their lifetime results in, at the end, Nothing! How wrong they are for the end of one life signals the beginning of a new one, far more productive than the one they are leaving behind!

When a person is shall we say nearing the time when they will soon depart from this Earth, they cast their minds back over the years and try and take stock of them! Wondering perhaps where they went wrong at such and such a time and perhaps where did all those plans go to that in their youth were so strong and hopeful! Then they begin to wonder what next? If they believe in the "after life" they perhaps get somewhat apprehensive. It is something that they know precious little about. They have their theories and wonder if there's any truth in what they have heard and perhaps read! One thing is certain though, there is no escaping the fact that when it is their time to "go" they surely will and there's no denying that! So what will this new life be like? Better than the last one they hope and what is it that will be required of them when they embark upon this section of their long journey back to where they started out from?!

They have been told or read that how they have behaved while living upon the earth will be taken into consideration, as if good living is a passport to eternal bliss and if their lives have been somewhat selfish and self centred then woe betide them, there's a price to be paid if they wish to enter what they think of as Heaven! How wrong they are! W are not judged and separated into various categories that our previous existence warrants! No! God does not exact a price for you to enter into his Holy domains! It is You who do that with your own judgment of yourselves! But stop! Do you really know how to judge yourself? Would you not try and skip over what you felt were the unpleasant parts of your past life and perhaps exaggerate those points that you thought were good? So who best to be the judge of your life just past?!

Well we can tell you! It is all those who you have come into contact with all through that previous life! No, they do not sit in judgment of you, but you are shown in a picture form of how you have affected them by your actions and yes how they too have affected you by theirs! This then is the moving picture of your life's journey! This "film" as it were is the one you have made. You have been the director, the actor, the playwright, you in fact are responsible for the finished product! Now comes the real time for reflection and assessment of the past and believe me you will not only be surprised but astonished at what has made your life your own epitaph!

Things that you had completely forgotten about are there upon the screen for you and you alone to view! You are not subjected to be part of an audience. This film is yours and only seen by you! You will find that gestures and thoughts and actions have all played their part in creating the you that you are ! People who you hardly knew are there. Perhaps you were kind to them in passing. Just a word or a smile or an understanding thought made all the difference to them. You have forgotten but not them. You made a difference to their lives and they can now show you their gratitude. It was all those little gestures that eventually have made your life what it is! Then there were the mistakes, but were they? When viewed now you can see they were perhaps stepping stones along life's path. And a so called mistake can result in a positive good result! Not all mistakes are bad you know, just an error of judgment at a particular time. But perhaps it was for the best for you went down another path that altered that part of your life for the better! At the time you perhaps hadn't seen it in that light. But now you can see how those actions altered your perspective and you grew in stature without even realising it! People that have come and gone all leaving a mark upon your life as you did upon theirs! So you can see now how you have lived your life and really it hasn't been such a bad one after all has it? Some of your "errors" shall we say, did have unfortunate repercussions, but on the whole the positive far outweigh the negative results, and you emerge as a person that on the screen that you see, you begin to admire and yes rather like! You have made your mark in life even if you didn't think you had. That film that you have been viewing has turned out rather well hasn't it? You have learned lessons along the way that will now stand you in good stead. Nothing has been wasted, so looking back at that life of yours, the good points and perhaps the not so good ones, have all made you what you are now! Are you satisfied with what you have seen? Are you now ready to proceed with your new life here in the Spirit World? You can't alter what has been but you can profit by what has been shown to you, so that your new life will be more productive in every way. The film has come to an end. Will you come away from it a better person than when you first sat down to view it? I'm sure you will. It's time to begin a new one, for the old one now finished has been relegated to the ash can, finished completely and no longer needed. It's work has been done. A new chapter has been planned and you the actor are about to begin with a fresh scenario, are you ready?

We are now waiting to greet you as are all of your loved ones and the ones who are to be your fellow actors in this new play of yours called "LIFE!"

Chapter 22

Three score years and Ten! A number that with today's population does not hold much water! For the life span has increased somewhat since that quotation was originally uttered! But do these extra years teach you anything more we wonder? Or do you perhaps find those added years a burden and not a blessing? Difficult to say for everyone is different in their outlook. No two people view that added bonus with the same thoughts! So we will leave that subject and just say that what life teaches you does have a bearing on where you will find yourself once you have adjusted to the life in the Spirit World! You already know about the relieving of your life and what you have to do about the readjusting once you have, shall we say, "come to terms" with what has been needed on your part, regarding what atonements that you need to do before you are able to start out upon your new lifestyle and cycle! For not all those who have come over, shall we say, are to remain here on a permanent basis! In other words they may just be here on a temporary, shall we say, "visa" awaiting their return once more to the plane of Earth, for more lessons that are needed before that wheel of life can be dispensed with! Those we will not talk about, it is those who are now here, on what we have said a permanent basis, that are of our interest at the present moment!

You have spent a lifetime upon Earth and do the lessons of that lifetime have any relevance to your new one on the Spirit realm?! Well yes and no! For once those lessons have been evaluated you can now go forward. And where is that you wonder? You will find yourself with what we call "like minded persons". You will naturally gravitate to them and they to you so you will already have friendships in the making! and these can be lifelong or shorter depending on your progress! Nothing stands still. We are all progressing even if we do not quite understand that we are. It is only when you look back and reassess what you have learnt that you begin to see a pattern forming. This is the pattern of your future existence! Your life in fact, or more precise your lives to come! When you leave the Earthplane behind you also leave a lot of the memories that you have gathered while there! Some are relevant now, other scan be discarded for they have served their purpose. Gradually your Earth time experiences will fade and your journey upon that plane will be as naught! You may think now what a pity! But believe me your new life's cycle far outweighs the earth one. It has served its purpose and it is the one you are now living that is the important one for your evolvement in the upward spiral!

What we are telling you is that you may not necessarily be with those that were your companions, family or acquaintances, for as we have told you, we do not all progress at the same pace! You may be reunited with some of them later. That all depends upon their rate of progress. But you see things in a completely different way now and previous attachments are viewed as they should be! With detachment if you like! We are trying to tell you that what was felt upon the Earthplane is seen now for what it was! And we are not denigrating those feelings that you had, we are just putting them in their right perspective! Which is what you will do believe us on that subject!

So as we have said, new friendships formed, you are now part of the group of your choice, that will take you forward and upward as well as "inward"! But don't think that you have deserted your previous earthbound companions, you will most certainly come into contact with them, probably at social gatherings and the suchlike, for life does go on you know and they are just as preoccupied with their own lives as you are! And remember you will be viewing things differently so do not think in terms of the Earth life now! Things do not standstill as we have said before! Progress is ever ongoing for all of us and of course that means you upon the Earthplane as well!

We know that attachments upon Earth are very real and they are here as well, make no mistake about that, but as we have said your views are different here and that is as it should be! Just learn to accept that what is normal here, if viewed from Earth you perhaps could not understand its full impact to our life's cycle!

So much for you to try and accept, but don't hurry when you are thinking about it, take your time and come to your own conclusions! We can only tell you how we find things. You may see them quite differently. Just remember there's room for all points of view, wherever you are! We feel that this discourse should end here and at a later date we will tell you about the areas in which you will live and how they will affect your lifestyle.

Chapter 23

What can we tell you that would stimulate your thoughts? So much has been said and yet so much has been left unsaid! Is there a reason for this you wonder? Well yes there is little Brother, for if we were to tell you all that there is to know, and let me hasten to say we are not in possession of those elusive truths by any means, where would you be? Any wiser? Or at a standstill waiting for something more to whet your appetite! You see dear friend, we, that is all of us, can only as it were take in just so much, at any given period[You gradually "work up" to a point where you can say in all honesty "I do want more knowledge I am ready for it"]But are you dear friend? We cannot judge for ourselves how we are progressing , that is the prerogative of the Teacher! A true teacher knows just when to impart more knowledge that will stimulate the pupil into not only asking for more but will be able to see just how far he has advanced and, yes, just how little he really does know! That then is the sign what the Teacher has been waiting for. Progress in any worthwhile field of discovering has to be paced for the pupil concerned! Too much too soon and you could easily take two backward steps! Your very apt saying "Rome wasn't built in a day" has so much sense in it! Be patient, be diligent and your efforts will be rewarded. That is a promise that we can tell is the truth. Do not fear that you are not progressing and here we speak generally, when you feel that you cannot actually see progress! Progress starts from within. We can see even if you cannot and believe us when we say that your spirit is well aware of any progress made, for it affects that "body" as well as the physical.

Life is a succession of up's and down's, setbacks and moves forward. That is what it is all about. The thing to remember is that any setback can be not a stumbling block, but a crutch to help you on your upward journey. Always look on the positive side. Never the negative! You can always turn what might at first look like a setback into a forward motion. Never be daunted, for everything that you experience upon the Earthplane has a purpose! Learn to see it in that light and you will find that suddenly life becomes more meaningful in every way. To your astonishment, things fall into place, almost as if by magic! The magic is your perception and acknowledgement, that the lessons of life are taking you along the pathway of understanding you begin to see a pattern emerging in your life. One that God has had a hand in weaving even if you are not conscious of it[Don't believe in Fate. You are the Masters of it not its servants! You decide your own fate! It has NOT been decided for you or against you!]

We sometimes like to think "Oh! That's fate, what can I do about it?" and the "do about it" is said in a negative voice instead of a positive assertion of "What can I do about it?" Same words but with a different interpretation. And what person do you think will become the winner in this race against Fate!? You decided to come to this Earth because you knew that there were lessons to be learnt that could not be learnt elsewhere! So you see you really are not only the instigators of your so called Fate, but you are also the ones who can be victorious when "it" seems to be about to engulf you! There is always a "way out" if only you step back and view it in its right perspective. As if you were viewing someone else's fate and not your own! That way you can be objective and make the correct decision that affects your life and yours only even if the decision that you make does indirectly affect others. Make the right one and everything will fall into place. Believe that for it is the Truth!

Life upon Earth is for your benefit to help you to understand just where you stand in the scheme of things. You are an important part of this gigantic jigsaw that we call Life. Everyone has their rightful place and when eventually the whole picture is completed the true artist will be seen in all His glory, the one you call God and that word can be translated into any culture you care to name. It makes no difference to the Almighty what you call Him. A name is just a name. It all depends upon the one who is saying it and if you feel what you are saying and by feel we mean with love then you are a part of that One upon High and no one can deny you that right. For it is given by Him and Him alone. Love the universal currency that will take you anywhere and is accepted without question!

For Love is the bank that is open to all, you can open an account at anytime and the interest on that account just grows and grows. The more you take out the more you can put in! You will never be poor. Believe that the Spirit will get richer and richer and one day you will see how your love account has grown. Go forward from this day in Love and understanding. We leave you here and may the Blessings of the One on High be upon you and those who you love.

Chapter 24

Where do we go to when it is our time to leave this Earth behind? In other words the death of the mortal body but the release of the Spirit that has been somewhat entombed within the physical body while it dwelt upon the Earthplane! Now what does that tell you about the "Spirit Body"? It is that "it" is the real one, the immortal one that cannot die! It may change its appearance from time to time or more appropriately from sphere to sphere, but it is still that same Spirit that you have accepted as the "real you". While upon Earth because of its denseness and its cycles of birth and death the Spirit has not been able to be its complete self. As we have said the death of the physical body means the complete release of the Spirit. Do not be confused when we say "Spirit Body" for it is not a body in the sense that you think of as a body that is a physical one! There is Not another actual body residing in spaces left over in the physical one! Contrary to what many people think is the case! There wouldn't be room enough to accommodate two bodies in the one shell! Spirit though when it is on its natural plane of existence takes on the form of the physical vehicle that it inhabited upon Earth It is only as it were a familiar form of reference that can be identified by others, known and unknown if you can follow what is being said!

"Spirit" is shall we say an unknown quantity! It has a form and yet it can be formless! Paradox yes! But then you are looking at what we have said from a physical and material point of view and Spirit can not be judged by those standards! Spirit is the product of "Mind" and Mind is a subsidiary of what you upon Earth term your "Soul" which to you is an unknown quantity for "it" is what the Almighty has created as part of his "visible self" and so it has within itself untold powers that it is unaware of in its original state! That is why the Earthplane has been designated as a training ground, but because Soul is that part of the Divinity it cannot as it is dwell upon that lower plane. Its vibrations are too fine for that purpose. That is why it "creates" not only a physical vehicle but also various other vehicles or bodies if you wish to call them that which can when needed convey to Soul what it requires to stimulate its latent powers into positive action!

This all may sound complicated but in reality it is Not! It is rather difficult to explain the procedure in material language but it is a form of communication that extends through each of these so called bodies. Like an electric current that when the switch is thrown it becomes "live". That way all the information that has been gleaned from not only the one upon Earth, but also those other entities that reside upon the various planes of the higher understanding they all contribute in their own way to Soul's expansion of who and what it is and more importantly "Why it is"! It takes many, many lifetimes or incarnations which incidentally are not just confined to the Earthplane as so many people think. For incarnations take place upon all spheres of known existence and you notice we have said "known existence". That is because we are not in possession of knowledge about other planes or spheres that exist beyond our known senses! You see dear friends, we do NOT know everything in spite of the length of your time scale that we have been in existence! So you see you have not only much to learn but also many lives to live before you even reach our mode of habitation! But even Eternity is but a loose word to try and explain the unexplainable! That is in physical and material terms! Believe us though when we say that we all live in Eternity, just exclude your mortal body in that statement, for it is only Spirit that can be called Eternal and even that is not certain! For Spirit undergoes many changes in its "form" on its journey back to its source which you know of as Soul which even then is not the real end of its journey for Soul is then ready to start out upon its final journey that will take it back to its Divine Beginning and here we have to cease for we do not know how and what and where that takes place. That information has been withheld from us and for very good reasons if you care to think about it! And that also goes for you dear friend up on the lower sphere called Earth!

Your final destination as it is also for us, is a long, long, long way off If you are measuring time as you know it, which of course does not apply to those Higher Realms where past, present and future are all ONE! Time is timeless as is the Creator of all that there is! Do not try to understand for it is a mystery that must remain as one until you are ready for enlightenment! Should we perhaps say "all in good time?" and leave it at that! We hope that you will now be able to view Spirit in its new light. "it" is still you that is the recognisable you and yet it is fundamentally different because of its density or rather lack of it. For if you at present were to "see" Spirit in its true light you could not quite understand what it is that you are beholding.

You will when you too are dwelling upon the realms of Spirit which to you will seem like an illusion for all is not what it may appear to be and yet it is a reality, a reality of the Spirit!

Learn to accept that not all of what is told you can always be thought of as the whole truth! It is in part, but you are only shown or taught what it is deemed you can assimilate and judge for yourself! Remember that everything about life or lives apply to you for you are the one who is living them and learning from them! Accept, reject and then accept once more when you have learned how to use your inner perception which quite often is at variance with your outward one. But it is in the inner one that is the correct one for that is the one that is guided by your own "Spirit Consciousness!"

Farewell dear Spirits and Earth Friends for you are one in essence and that essence is from the One on High, the one we are all part of. The part that is sometimes known as the flesh made manifest! May the Blessings of those upon High be upon you and within you, now and forever more.

Chapter 25

Let your pen speak for us clear friend. There is so such turmoil in your World today, people are questioning just where is it heading to? You are witnessing global changes, that are beginning to frighten you, for you are seeing Nature behaving in an erratic fashion, but fear not brethren all has been planned! You think how can this form of chaos be planned? Well it has to be kept in check, there is no way that Nature will be allowed to disrupt the plans that the almighty has for this your World! It may seem for a while that 'all hell has been let loose'. But that is because your World has become somewhat 'unstable'. It is like a boiling kettle! It has to let off steam, otherwise it will blow its top off! And we are not speaking metaphorically! It is a fact. Deep, deep within the globe of yours there boils a cauldron of gasses that have to be allowed to give vent to their overpowering surplus energy! As yet Man is not in a position to harness this force and believe us it is a force but it will be harnessed one day by those that will come after you, long, long after we say! You World has to undergo a lot of changes before complete stability can be achieved! This is all 'normal' it may not seem like it to those who are living through this change, but it is, believe that. There is so much that 'goes on' within the bowels of your Planet that are at present not understood by your scientific bodies! Your waters for one thing are beginning to 'warm up' in areas hitherto thought of as cold and stable! You have had your ICE age and you have also had your periods of 'heat', this is one of those periods, but it will not be as drastic as is thought.

There will of course be what you will term catastrophes, but that is inevitable when change in Natures patterns take place! You are going to witness certain upheavals in your land masses that will radically change the contours of some of your continents! Somewhere in the area of New Zealand and Australia, new islands will be formed that will join up together making a new continents. In the tropics you will find less humidity, their climate will become less hot and populations will alter. In the areas of the North and South Poles there will arise or rather will be made visible large land masses that hitherto have been uninhabitable for humans and animals! There is within these lands huge deposits of minerals that will become available to man, and some of these are as yet unknown substances, but they are just waiting to be 'tapped into'. These deposits represent 'energy' vast amounts of it. Not in the form of liquid fuel but of a form of foliage type fossil that will be used to harness the Suns energy, it will be able to be 'stored' and used like your Electricity, but not in quite the same manner as you understand electricity. It can be used for all forms of transportation and also for providing not only light and warmth but also a form of 'food' quite unlike anything you know about today! This 'food' as we will call it will be 'medicinal' and will cure many ailments of the body that have been thought incurable! in the past. Unfortunately, owing to the change in Natures habits there will be certain diseases that will take hold for a while of the

Earths population, this will result in a form of 'infertility' of both sexes! Your populations are to become somewhat dissipated, you have far too many for this planet to sustain in complete harmony with its natural resources!

This all sounds very drastic to you no doubt, but it will only come about gradually and not 'overnight' so to speak! Nations will adjust to this, they will have to for there is no alternative for them. Food will become scarce unless you stop all this tampering with what is termed 'Nature'! You are altering the balance, though it is not too late to reverse this change if you have the will to do so! You need to 'pull in your belts' so to speak, your bodily consumption of food far outweighs your bodies needs for a healthy lifestyle. In time this balance will be restored and you will find that the populations that will follow will be 'leaner', and finer in every way, taller, more muscular, and will use their brain power in a way that at present is not understood! You can generate your own heat and cold in a way that would not necessitate your primitive way of using fossil heat power! But that is a long way off I'm afraid. You will have you learn how to use your brain power to overcome what is lacking at present. Schools will teach the young how thought can be used to manipulate what at present requires physical exertion! There is much more that the generations of the future will be able to do, that would be impossible for those living today to accomplish.

This will all require a radical way of thinking, for thought will be used as a 'tool' and not as it is at present, most of your thought power is frittered away in idle 'thought' and not used as it is intended to be! You will learn eventually and your world will become a better place to live in, for you and your Spirit will be joined as never before and so you will view the whole of life's existence in a completely different way, you will be in 'tune' with Nature, in other words with your 'God'! So look forward and not backward at what has been, but what can be and what 'will be' achieved when man learns that he is part of the Universal creator and as such he is responsible for all of his actions! And not just for himself but for all peoples everywhere!

We tell you these things even though they do not apply to you upon Earth, at this period of its evolution! But that does not mean that you cannot make a start to better your understanding of what God is all about! Work with Him! In other words work with Nature and not against her! That way all of this forthcoming upheaval can be seen in its true perspective, it may be unpleasant for those living through it, but in the 'long run' it will all be for the best. Think of those who will one day follow you and who knows you may even be one of those! That should make you think and dare we say make you act in a more positive manner in your everyday living! It could well be your future that we have talked about in this nights discourse! We will leave you on that note, and please go along with the flow of life's tide, do not fight against it, compromise is the word, you can make a difference if you really want to!

Chapter 26

You begin to wonder what more can be said regarding life upon the so called Spirit plane and yet when you stop to think about it you say to yourself 'have I really been told anything'? Well little Brother, yes, you have but not everything! There are reasons, for one thing we don't know everything that there is to be known about our world of the Spirit! That probably surprises you but it is a fact and a truth! So often when people on the Earth think about Spirit they imagine all sorts of things, usually things that they consider would suit them! But is life upon your Planet like that? The answer not a definite No, but shall we say 'sometimes', you have to work for what you consider your happiness and well being, it does not come about without effort on your part, well dear friends it is just the same on our sphere! Nothing shall we say 'falls into your lap!' and really why should it, when you think about it! Anything that is worthwhile, is worthwhile not 'fighting' for, but 'striving' for. We are no different here, we too have what you call our 'ups and downs' and yes, we even have what you call 'an off day'! Now, that really will surprise you! 'an off day'. How can a spirit have an off day? Well think about it, we still have a mind that governs our actions and thoughts! Not everything goes to plan shall we say! For we are individuals and individuals don't all behave in the same way do they? We have our preferences in all things and that does include people as well! So as upon Earth we do not expect everything to 'run smoothly'. But, and here we stress the point, we do not get upset when things do not work out how we hoped that they would! We do not hold 'grudges'! we may even dislike someone, as they may equally feel the same about us! But that is all, we either avoid them or better still we try and understand them and when you do that with good intent, then quite often the feelings alter, you see the real person and not just what you think you see! Its all so much like the Earthplane isn't it? Except that we think more deeply about everything and everyone! If you upon the Earth were to do the same, you would find that your lives would be so much happier and stable in every way, so you see we lead a pretty 'normal' life here, not quite the same as you do, for we have so much more freedom, not only of movement, but of thought and yes, actions! Though do not think that life here is like one long holiday for it is not! We have our commitment and not only to our family units! There is plenty of worthwhile activity, what you might call 'service to the community'!

You are not, shall we say, expected to take up a service activity, its all up to you, but you will find that most spirit people are anxious to be of 'service', it is one way of showing that they are now committed to this new way of life! For it is a new way of life, believe us. If we say there are still lessons to be learnt, do not be daunted, for life itself is one long lesson, whichever way you look at it, it was upon Earth only you didn't perhaps see it in that light. The word 'lesson' always conjures up thoughts of teachers and classrooms! Well, its not so here and yet, there are, shall we say adult classrooms, where you learn what this spirit life is for and how you fit into this life! And also what will 'come after' when your lives upon this sphere have served their purpose! Lessons here are very, very instructive, for you are shown how others live upon our Sphere of learning. The 'films' for want of a better word are not only three 'dimensional' they allow you to actively partake of a particular life style, you experience it at first hand so to speak. That way you get to understand other cultures that do exist upon our world! We are not all the same, we never were upon Earth and that still applies here, so you see you will have much to re-learn about not only life, but people as well!

You may even wish to take up a service activity in one of these other areas, you are not restricted in any way in what you choose to do with this, your new life! There really is so much for you to look forward to once you have left your physical body behind and are now in your own permanent Spirit one, which you really have always been, without actually knowing it! Have you not wondered sometimes when you have had shall we say a vivid and realistic dream, where you have visited some far off place that you know you have never actually been to in 'real lie'. Buildings quite different, landscapes unknown, people you meet and sometimes talk to, that really are to you complete strangers? Well, you have been in your sleep state where one day you will recognise those places and you will find that they do really exist and are not just products of your imagination! You see dear friends you are nearer to the a Spirit world that you realise, and one day, a long way off I'm afraid, Spirit and Earth will be in unison and so you will live as it were upon both planes at the same time! Same life different existence! Time and Space will no longer be of any importance, for everything will be in the now! But that as we have said is a long way off as far as the Earth world is concerned! But it is something that we look forward to as a reality of the future!

We feel that we will leave you there. There will be more for you one day, when we feel it is time for more knowledge to be imparted to you.

Chapter 27

We are going to create for you a journey of the mind. Yours and Ours! We will actually do the travelling but you will benefit from our observations. This journey is to be not only one that is informative but also one of instruction! We will begin, we would like to tell you to close your eyes, but as this is not practical we say to you, write as you are impressed and then when this journey and discourse has been completed, read over what has been written and then record it on your little machine and then you can close your eyes and listen to where you have been and what you have seen!

So dear friend let us start our journey! And we start it from the top of that little hill yonder. There! We are now above the landscape, looking down from our height we can see streams of crystal clear water, running down the hillside, and pouring into a lake that has all the colours of the rainbow within it, the lake stretches into the distance and upon it we see small craft bobbing about in the gentle breeze, as we pass over them the occupants wave to us for we truly are a spectacular sight to those upon the water. We resemble at this stage a flock of iridescent plumaged birds, that sparkle in the sunlight, we circle the lake and head for the distant mountain, which is tall and its peak is covered in what looks like a golden canopy, it remains like that always, and at night time, it glows, giving off a soft and beautiful light that illuminates the surrounding countryside. We hover over the summit as if to get our bearings, but we do know the direction we are to take, we glide gently down into the valley below and as we touch the ground we are once again our own light bodies of habitation! The valley is dotted with small buildings, pretty little dwelling places, we pass along well kept streets or rather path ways for this really is what you upon Earth call a 'hamlet'. We are greeted with smiles and the children play alongside of us as we walk we come to the edge of the valley and beyond stretches a vast savanna like landscape. We proceed on a foot or rather we glide over the terrain, as we approach the other side, we then look down at a sight that is awe inspiring for this is one of the many schools of learning, they stretch as far as eye can see, there are colleges, universities and large buildings that house what you might consider libraries. These are all of the technical variety for much study and learning is carried on here! And this studying is not for the benefit of those upon this planet, but for other planets that are in our orbit which includes your Earthplane! Inventions and suchlike are created here and perfected as well, before they are 'handed over' to those for whom they are intended! Sadly some of these peaceful inventions are turned around and you upon Earth see the results in your lands of War!

Let us move on, we see many students and each school or university has their own colour scheme, this actually denotes what the students are studying! For colour is a living vibrant force and the students are shown how to manipulate colour as a 'tool' that can create what is required! You see little friend 'thought' here is something very potent and is not used for idle speculation. It is taught that with proper guidance, thought can transform what might be termed 'liquid clay' into something worthwhile and if required permanent in it construction!

Our buildings are not only things of beauty, they are actual places where people live and 'work'. All this has to be taught to those with an aptitude for this form of work experience! Everything is carefully thought out, before being given permission to be built, we are very orderly here and what may seem to be random structures are nevertheless planned and are 'overseen' by those whose 'job' it is! All sounds familiar to you I expect, well of course it is! For buildings, houses, etc have to be built to last for as long as they are needed, we can't just say 'building be' and it does so, all by itself! This is a practical world as well as being one of great beauty and variety!

We travel on once more and come to a wide ocean, so once again we assume our bird like camouflage and soar into the heights and then we skim over the placid water and alight once more on the firm land. Ahead of us we can see gleaming the spires and minaret's of the Holy places for this part of our globe is given over to all the known and unknown religious cultures, each building and that word covers all of the structures that are considered Holy! This is a place where all those who are interested in the history of Religion can learn all about its basis, going right back to primitive man and yes, even before He took residence upon the Earth, for there were cultures and very advanced ones that settled upon your Earth from outer space! Some returned to their source, while others languished upon Earth and eventually disappeared leaving no trace, and yet some will be discovered in the future bought to the surface by earthquakes and volcanoes! And even from under the seabed when it decides to erupt, which it will, in the not too distant future!

But to return, this is a Holy place, that echo's to the chanting of monks and the calling of the prayers for the faithful and many others! Here all religions are tolerated, they agree to differ and that means complete harmony. People just wander in and out of the Holy places and absorb what is being given out, and you may be surprised to realise how alike they all are, when they are understood! For God is Universal whatever some people may think, He belongs to no one and yet He belongs to us all!

We rest in this area for quite some time, for to us it is like coming home once more and we are reluctant to leave it, but leave it we must for it is time for us to bring you back to what you think of as reality! But is it we wonder? Not to us any more for we know what reality is, and it is not on your little sphere of uncertainty! We hope that when you listen to yourself you will perhaps understand just a little bit more of this World that awaits you! And believe us, there's so much more for you to know about, before it is your time to vacate the Earthplane and really begin to live in the Real World!

Chapter 28

Look around you Brother! What do you see? Yes, we know, the grass, the flowers, the trees, in fact all that lives! But that is not all, for even things that you may call inanimate have life! Not perhaps as you understand that word but it is a form of life! And we will tell you just why! Because of the denseness of your planet there is much that is not observed by those living upon it! You may not be aware but everything and we stress that word, everything, has what might be termed a force field that not only surrounds it but actually feeds it! And that little Brother not only goes for you but for all the Humanities and we include ourselves in that statement! This field of force is pure, pure energy and is not diluted in any way. If you could see as we can and do, you would be amazed at not only its power but its colour as well! You probably have never thought of Electricity as having vibrant colours, but it has! And when it is in connection with the human body it takes on many colours that are sometimes called your aura! When the force field is to be used for human activity it is somewhat like a vaporous substance. A mist, made up of millions of almost invisible particles, all vibrating in unison and yet each one separate with its own light force which as we have said is life force from the universal source of all life substance. This really is a living source, something like your reservoirs upon Earth and incidentally it is just like upon Earth, it needs 'topping up' from time to time! For mental energy uses up a great deal of electrical discharges and must be replaced as soon as possible!

You wonder sometimes why it is that you feel, shall we say, 'under the weather' a very apt saying! That is because your 'batteries' have become 'clogged up' with waste from your ceaseless activity, both mental and physical! 'They' need cleaning out, so that the life force can once more flow into the body unhindered! Physical man wastes a lot of his natural energy because he has no knowledge of how to either conserve it or use it constructively!

One day he will have learnt how to use his thought waves to his own and others advantage, but until that comes about he will go on floundering and dissipating this vital life giving energy!

We upon the realms of light know how this energy field works and we can harness it for our own use! We can, as it were, move and assemble large objects with absolutely no effort whatsoever! This was known about, upon your Earthplane many, many civilisations ago, but sadly misuse led to a deterioration in their physic abilities and they lost the power that had been latent within them! Perhaps one day it may return when man has turned once more to his Spiritual counterpart for advice and this time not to ignore it! As we have hinted at, all life forms and those called inanimate are surrounded by electrical currents, in fact that is what the whole Universe and those that inhabit it and here we are speaking of the planets and worlds and yes, all of that so called debris left over from disappearing worlds and galaxies no longer in existence and have been long, gone before your world came to be populated! Everything, yes, everything is made up of Electrical currents or wavelengths, these can be positive or negative! And as such can attract or repulse one another! Worlds have been known to collide because of this attraction which of course is to their detriment! There is so much unseen activity going on not only upon your Earth, but in the Oceans that surround your land masses and the sky that you think of as blue! We can see what you cannot, for to you these electrical discharges are not entirely visible! You may see the 'results' sometimes and they can be catastrophic, we see the origins of what is to take place! These of course do not impinge upon our world of thought for we do not come within the orbits of its destruction! We can view you from a safe distance and we are thankful for it! Believe us! You now wonder if we too experience anything like you do upon the Earth plane? Well we do have what you term weather, but it is shall I say ordered and kept in check. There are, we are informed, areas right on the perimeter of our known world that do sometimes experience shall we say the 'left over' of some of your catastrophic events, they find them quite exhilarating for they are an uncommon sight and do no damage to our environment!

Electricity when it is untamed is very volatile and yes, to a certain extent unstable! You will in time learn how to harness all of this gigantic life force and bring in into subjection, but not yet I'm sorry to say. Though there are those upon your planet who are working towards that goal, but they are, so far, doing it somewhat in secret! They have to for various reasons! But there are those upon 'our side' of life who have perfected a way of controlling certain elements of this life force for electricity is not always the same as maybe thought. It varies not only in power but in density and certain colour spectrums can be used In the healing of some of your more prevalent diseases! You will see a break through in this field shortly and those who are responsible for it will have no idea where these ideas have come from! Our scientists do not need or require thanks for their efforts in trying to combat Earths diseases, just the knowledge that what they are doing goes some way to alleviate your problems. They do it with love as we all do when trying to help you our Brothers upon the Earthplane.

Remember then, that when you feel 'out of sorts' there is a very good reason. Look to the intakes of your food substances and see if what you are receiving is really of benefit to not just your bodily needs but also your Spiritual! And it is to that one that you should think of first. When Body and Spirit are in harmony then you are a healthy being, though do not immediately think that that is the only answer, for life is more complex than that, but it is a step in the right direction. Tune into your spiritual wireless, and try to absorb what it is that you are hearing. You will be surprised at the knowledge that you will get, for it will be coming from the Universal source of all knowledge and that is always the truth, even if it contradicts what you have always thought!

66

Chapter 29

Dear friends of the Earthplane, what is it that we can say to you that will hold your attention? So much has been written over the years about the Spirit World and those who dwell upon it, so what is it that we can say to you that is new? Well let us be honest, is anything new? Or is it just something that has been voiced before but now given a new slant on an old problem? People are anxious these days, they want to be told things that are not only going to alter their lives, but will give them a degree of comfort and hope for the future! All around them they see the fabric of their known society crumbling! Things that were considered permanent and binding are now looked upon as obsolete and yet those who profess that they know the answer to all of these problems cannot give you a straight answer. What they tell you does just not hold water, it is full of holes and any truths that may be there are obscured by fancy rhetoric that when you start to try and unravel it you find you are back where you started, and none the wiser! But then what is wisdom? Usually it is just plain common sense! But we don't like to be told that do we? We want something out of the ordinary, something that fires the imagination! We want a truth that we have never heard before! But if it is a truth then we have heard it before but probably forgotten it in the clamouring for what we feel is something that no one else has got! We deceive ourselves, whether we realise it or not! For Truth when it is plain and unvarnished has always been there staring us in the face! It was given to us over two thousand years ago, by one who walked this earth spreading the news that God the Father is a God of love and not the vengeful deity of the Old Testament! He never was, how could he be when he brought us into being by love! And that really is all that you need to know! Love the kind that is not only Universal but is unselfish in every way! And how many people with a hand on their heart can honestly say that when they give love it is of the unselfish kind? Usually love is given with one hand held behind the back! And not as it should be with open arms outstretched to embrace all that need it!

When you look upon a cross with the figure of Jesus upon it, you see the pain and suffering of that mortal body, the nails tearing at the flesh, the head hung low on the breast, despair is what you see, and yet He came into the world to uplift you not to make you sad and unhappy! His whole mission was one of Hope and Love, love for all of humanity. So when you next look upon a cross, see not the arms impaled upon the wood, but see them outstretched and inviting you to go to Him in joy and thanksgiving for showing us the way that we should live, always with arms outstretched ready to embrace a lost soul, never with arms folded against the chest, defiant and uncaring! Jesus was a man of the people, he understood their needs for wasn't he, nay isn't he still the Son of the One on High? His message was simple, 'love ye one another' and 'all things shall be added unto you'! They are when you live by that simple principle, love! There is nothing else you need to know either about life or death, for death is but the open door to everlasting life, we all have to go through it sometime, and just think of the glorious life that awaits you on the other side of that door? Its not a dark and sinister one, its a golden gate of hope and freedom from all of Earths woes and yet we are here upon this Earth to learn and yes, teach as well, for if you learn the lessons of life you are in a position to share your knowledge with your fellow man who is also a fellow traveller on the same path as you, back to the source of all love and understanding namely Our Father God who is not just in Heaven but within each and every one of his dear creations! We are all Brothers, one big family of Nations, never look for the differences between us, look for the similarities, for they far outweigh those so called differences, which usually are just misunderstandings and nothing more! Jesus did not and does not belong to just one race of people. He, like his Father, belongs to all of us, call him what you will, it makes no difference. God, Jehovah, Allah, they are just names given by Man to try and identify with. God needs No Name, look into the face of your Brother and there you will see the face of God! Look into the mirror and there you will see the reflection of the One on High. You are that reflection for you are the face of God, we all are, it doesn't matter if the colour of the skin is dark or fair, for colour is just pigmentation, just a camouflage that lets us know we may look different but beneath the colour we are all the same! And when you look at another being with love then remember that love is colour blind! Just as God is!

So you see dear friends there is nothing new is there? You had the answer within you all the time and that answer is so simple that it gets overlooked time and time again, it is just that one word love and that really means love one another and that really is all that you need to know about life. So cease looking for an alternative for nothing can replace love. It is the gift that is bestowed upon us by our Father in Heaven and is given freely to all of His children everywhere.

Go forward from this day on, in love and friendship for all that you come into contact with for each day you are meeting your maker in the person of your fellow human being.

Chapter 30

You wonder what on Earth can we talk to you about, when it seems that by all accounts we should have exhausted all that we can say, either regarding life upon Earth or life in the Realm of the Spirit! If we were to say that trying to understand all that there is to know on these two subjects is well nigh impossible do you think that that would be a good enough explanation? There is so much that is either said of left unsaid, that you begin to wonder just where does the truth lie?! Well let us say 'in-between' does that make any sense to you? Well it is the truth believe that! Nothing is ever just black and white, but is the grey areas in-between that hold most of the so called knowledge that you are hoping to hear about! But dear friend, do we know what those grey areas contain? We have our ideas and they are just ideas for if the truth is known no one ever knows the full story of life in those two fields of human activity! You can be told one thing only to have it taken away from you with a fresh idea from another quarter! So what are we trying to tell you? That you must not accept everything that you read or have been told at face value! It is not to say that you have been, shall we say, lied to, for that would not be the truth, it is just that everyone looks at things from their point of view and experience and so it may well be quite difficult to find two versions on the same subject that entirely agree with each other!

Not to say that they are deliberately misleading, just that either version can be seen as a truth and you notice we have said 'a truth'. We did not qualify that statement as the whole truth! That dear friends has to be thought upon by you and if it seems to strike a chord, then of along with it,....for the time being! You think that that sounds ambiguous! Well I suppose you are right but remember that Truth in one age can easily be overturned in another! And yet that was the Truth then so how can it not be at that later date? Well let us say that Truth when seen as a reflection in a mirror can easily be distorted by the refraction of the light and yet it still remains the Truth! You begin to wonder if what you have been told or always thought of as a truth have been flawed in some way and you are now left with questions that seem unanswerable! Not so, not so, just use your brain, or rather use that thinking apparatus called your Mind! Sift through everything that you know of as the Truth and somewhere you will find for yourself what you are searching for! The truth shall we say is within each and every one of us! Learn to see it for what it is! Truth can be and is many things and so is open to many interpretations! It is entirely up to you how you chose to see it! Remember though, that as we have said truth can be changed even though it remains the truth! Each day can bring a different slant on what you think about things! A word, a hint, a passage in a book, all can suddenly alter you previous conception of what you thought of as Truth!

What we are telling you dear friends is think for yourselves, you may not always come up with the right interpretation, but at least you have tried in your own way to try and understand what at times must seem well nigh impossible!

What it all 'boils down to' is that Truth is very difficult to verify as a Truth at all times! Like the weather it varies! So be prepared within yourself to accept that truth about anything and yes, everything, is, to put it mildly, 'variable'. So even when we tell you what we think either about Earth life or that upon the Spirit plane, we are only speaking as we have found it, it is our variation and is as far as we can say the truth as we see it! You begin to think will I ever know the full truth about anything! Of course you will providing that you keep your thoughts flexible! We do hope that we haven't confused you too much, it is just that we want you to think for yourselves and make up your own minds about everything that you are studying! For life is a form of study is it not? Likewise the life that awaits you upon the Spirit plane. You will learn and adjust to it when you are here and no amount of conjecture on your own part can ever really satisfy your inner longings to know the whole truth about that future life. We will give you an honest account of how we find it, someone, somewhere else, perhaps in another book will tell you something quite different, don't dismiss it out of hand! It is just another variation of the truth as it has affected them! And as it will affect you as a thinking person. Never give up this desire of yours to know the truth just be prepared to accept that it may not always be as you think!

We feel that we will leave this subject now, don't be disheartened by what we have told you this night. Just like 'beauty' it is in the eye of the beholder!. We bid you farewell and May the Blessings of the One on High be with you all. Farewell Brother scribe, Farewell much for you to think upon.

Chapter 31

In your mind you have been wondering about those other worlds and planets that whirl around in your cosmos. You wonder if they are in any way inhabited by beings that you can identify with as human beings and if they are, are they anything like you upon Earth or have they advanced further up the scale of Evolution and would you appear to them as somewhat of a primitive form of species! Well dear friend what do you think? That you, upon planet Earth are somewhat primitive in your outlook even regarding each other and by that we mean those other nationalities! Unfortunately you haven't yet learnt the lesson of tolerance and the art of living and let live! Until you have truly accepted that principle and yes, lived by it, you will never be accepted on equal terms by those other outer life forms that your scientists are hoping to come across with their rather antiquated transport machines! They probably think that they are what you term 'state of the art' which we find a most peculiar expression! If you could see what we have seen regarding those other planets you would soon realise how very backward you really are in comparison with those other inhabitants in outer space! You are not in their time scale for one thing, that is one of the reasons for their advancement, that you could come to terms with. If and it is a fairly big if you were able to view their cities, the way they are planned for the benefit of all and not for the favoured few you would come back to your war torn planet and know just how backward you really are! Their whole lifestyle is geared for the whole community, there is no such thing as class distinction, it is unheard of there, they would not even understand what you meant if you were to try to explain it to them! of course there are those who you would term 'are in authority' but that word is an earth one and does not explain the position of those who, shall we say, exercise it! For it is a cooperative form of authority, taking into consideration all aspects of what the society needs and requires! In fact everyone 'has a say' in anything that will affect all peoples! You would call this life force one of 'Utopian excellence'. That is not to say that people are not in possession of their own thoughts on any given subject, but they instinctively know what is best for the whole and abide by that. Now we have only dealt with shall we say 'one world' there are so many others and all equal in their treatment of each other! It seems its only your world that is out of step with what could be termed the normal way of life!

You wonder how it is that these inhabitants of these other worlds have reached this advanced stage in the evolutionary cycle. Were they like it originally or have they become through 'trial and error' this rather exalted state of living! Well let us say that they were born with this feeling of

71

understanding about each other, it has come somewhat naturally to them. You on the other hand, that is the Earth people have to learn that lesson the 'hard way'. It would seem that your nature is basically a hostile one that was needed in the beginning of Mans Sojourn upon the Earth planet for it is a somewhat hostile form of planet, all due to its rather dense 'make up' that is needed to keep it going! But eventually this will be altered, ever so gradually so as not to cause too much disruption which is very, very violent that is why you have so many earthquakes and volcanic eruptions! All I'm afraid very necessary if your Earth is to remain stable and not wander out of its planned orbit!

You will 'get there' one day, but not in the foreseeable future as far as we can tell! But then you do have Eternity on your side don't you? That is not to say that you can ignore the signs that you are now seeing all around your planet. You have to play your part in the evolution of this your world if you wish to become part of the Universal Brotherhood of all Mankind's! Start by bringing yourself into a form of 'subjection', in other words let your Spirit force be the guiding force in your lives! Doesn't matter whether you believe that you are primarily made up of Spirit essence or not, just learn the art of tolerance towards all other people! Regardless of race, colour or so called Religion! Once you begin to live like that then you will find that even your planet will respond in a like manner. Disease and poverty will become things of the past, for you will have learnt how to treat your planet in the right manner!

It can be done, if you really want to improve your lifestyles and bring them into line with those that we have talked about! What it boils down to is to bring back God into your everyday living, or shall we put it another way? Lead a 'good life' which amounts to the same thing really, you don't have to be 'pious' and pay lip service to what, to some, are outdated thoughts, just learn to live and let live and that goes for all people wherever they may live! Life is for living and living for each other, not selfishly, for self should not come into this equation!

Start with yourself! Analyse what it is that will make your and others lives 'livable'! Once all people begin to think in that way, then this world will cease being considered that dense and dark planet called Earth by others in those far off galaxies! For one day you must all come together, exchange 'ideas' and learn that living in harmony is the only real way to live a fulfilling life. Either here or maybe one day elsewhere! Think about it, it could come about, but only if you put your own house in order first and wait for others to contact you and then you will know that you have arrived and are part of this Brotherhood of all Mankind's that we have spoken about!

72

Chapter 32

How often do you, and here we talk of people in general, stop and think, where am I going to when its my time to depart this life? Most thinking people will say 'Why, Heaven of course' but have they really thought what they mean by that statement? If you were to ask them to explain it, they would probably shrug their shoulders and say 'Well, heaven is where we all go to when we die unless its to the other place! But still that does not explain what they have said and thought! and why is that? Well, no one has actually been there and come back, we know that there are people who have had near death experiences and they say about the tunnel of light and voices of loved ones who tell them they have to return to their earth bodies, which they do, and that does help them for they all say that they now have no fear of death for they know that there is life after this one ceases! But still, no positive confirmation of what Heaven is like, really like, it is all so vague and some people will brush it aside when they hear about it and put forth some scientific explanation that they have read somewhere that purports to be able to prove that it is all an hallucination! The same effect can be caused by drugs etc.! So what! That still is no real explanation of what it is that has actually happened to those people and there have been these experiences from all round the world and they are all basically the same. So there must be some truth in them mustn't there? When we hear or read about what these so called experts have to say on the matter, we just have to laugh, for we are the living proof that the life after death is a reality and not a myth! We know we are alive, and that we do actually live somewhere, what ever you like to call our place or plane of existence! But still we cannot convince the majority of the population that what we have just said is correct and the Truth. People Want to believe it, but there's always this nagging doubt, which of course is understandable, they want positive proof, the sort that you can handle as it were, before they will actually believe in its reality! Unfortunately the Church, and here we use the word in its broadest sense! The Church does not help much when people ask about what is loosely termed 'the after life'. They either imply that we are not meant to know, but trust that something like another life does exist, or that one day we will know! And they hope that that will satisfy the one who has asked the question! Now in the West there is the Spiritualist organisation or Church if you like, that does at least try to explain about the 'hereafter', though even they don't always give you what we would call a 'down to Earth' explanation! But at least they do try and should be commended for their efforts. Of course anything to do with what is termed the 'occult' has always been looked upon with suspicion and yet most people have a sneaking desire to know more, but hesitate to come into the open about it! Probably because they have been brought up in the so called orthodox fashion of what the Church calls

'Heaven and Earth' and so they tend to feel a little guilty if they query what they have always been told! But today the young people want to know more about what has for centuries been taboo! They search for a meaning to life and what may lie beyond this one that they are living upon Earth! Unfortunately there are numerous sects that spring up all trying to show the unwary the way to everlasting paradise! One to come! So they feel they are on to a good thing, because no one can say yea or nay when they say that Heaven awaits those who will accept what they are saying, and your passport to this Heaven is by way of what you contribute when asked to by your free will generosity!

Jesus said the only payment required was to lead as good a life as you can, believing in the Heavenly Father and loving one another in true universal love! But to so many people they would rather put a coin in the box instead of actually living what has been shown does work when truly put into practice! But it does require an effort, but its worth it, and you know it does, so why should it be so hard? Surely loving one another is far more productive than this ever increasing hate and distrust that seems to be the normal way of today's living! It all boils down to family ties! They don't seem to count for much these days do they? But that is where the stability of any Nation starts! It is the value of the family and the extended family of grandparents, aunts and uncles and yes, 'god parents'. Bring back those values of yesteryear when a neighbour really was a neighbour and a friend, a friend when you needed one, these days you have to search high and low before you can find one it seems! Teach your children the true values of life, the ones that God has given freely, the earth, the sky, the birds, the trees, all the living things that make life what it is! Not what you can see on your television screens, false lifestyles that rely upon how much money you can spend on trivialities that don't last from one season to the next!

Your wealth comes from the love of your family and not from what you can put in the bank! We see from our side the utter waste and futility of your lifestyles, they are not built upon from rock but upon shifting sand and you can see for yourselves what the outcome is! Stop! And think! There is still time for you to change your attitudes to make your world a fit place for everyone, yes everyone to live in! in harmony and peace! It must come about if you are to survive, think about it, and act upon it! Don't leave it to someone else for if you do it will never get done!

Your World can still be a beautiful place in which to live and learn and learn the lesson of how to live with one another in love and harmony, and remember it starts with the family, for aren't we all one big family whatever nation we think we belong to?! We should learn to forget nationalities and think of everyone as our Brothers, and when you do, then this is where your real Heaven starts and continues in your next realm of existence.

74

Chapter 33

People think about what is loosely termed the After Life, but they tend not to let their thoughts dwell too deeply in case the questions that they would like answers to will perhaps not be the ones that they wish to hear! And why is that you think? It is because it might mean that they will have to alter their lifestyle? They don't want to feel that that is the only answer that will not only satisfy them, but that is signifies the end of their sojourn upon the Earthplane! The only place that they can actually identify as Home and Reality! Understandable we agree, but one cannot forever put off that time when answers must result in a change of attitude, not only to live upon that planet but more importantly the one that is the continuation of it on the sphere that is associated with the word spirit! Too many people, especially those of the western hemisphere, the word Spirit makes them think of seances and the like, the 'unknown' the place that perhaps doesn't bear thinking about, for it spells the end of the known life that they have been living! How wrong they are if they did but know it! For the word Spirit should mean the release from bondage of the Earth body and the resumption of the interrupted life that they had upon that plane of the Spirit! Tell them that and they will say 'well why don't I remember that place if that is where I came from?' a question that needs to be answered and answered with the Truth! You don't remember because if you did, your mind would be so confused that you would not be able to accept this period of life upon this lower sphere, you would feel what is the justice of being taken away from a life on one sphere and made to take up another one on a planet that is not what they feel is 'home'! Yet it is a very necessary place where one can actually learn about 'life' granted it may seem to some what is the point of it if our real 'home' is upon the Spirit Realm! We have lessons to learn and that word makes one feel that they are back in a classroom and they don't like the sound of that! But dear friends 'life' is a classroom, it may not be seen in that light, but never the less it is true! To appreciate what our true home is, is the reason for leaving it in the first place! We then eventually come to the realisation that this one upon Earth is not the permanent one that we thought it was, that there is one that is the only real and permanent one and this earth one is but a reflection of they true one, the one to which we, as Spirit really belong to. It is only by being away from it that we can in time appreciate what our true home means to us! You will then argue that if we eventually go back to where we have come from, surely this earth time that we have spent away from it is rather a waste of time and effort! It may seem like that to some people, but it is a very necessary time that is spent upon Earth! We come into contact with situations that do not occur upon the Spirit Realm, it is all part of our 'character building' that is very necessary to our 'Spirit body' which though having a character it has not had the opportunity to explore its full potential That can only come about by a life upon this lower plane of existence! And we cannot fully appreciate that until we return once more to our home land in the Spirit Realm! Where we review our past incarnation upon Earth and we then see what that period has taught us about ourselves! For that is the prime reason for our earth life, it is to find out who we really are, but it seems that it is only when we leave it behind that we can actually see what that life has taught us. You will then say, 'well, what has it taught us that is of use to us back upon the spirit realm?' it has taught us that we are part of the human race! It should have taught us humility, unselfishness towards others and understanding of our relationship with our God and we can only do that by living upon Earth away from Him! If we learn the lessons that life teaches us, then we begin to see the reason why we are here and why we long to return to the source of all life the union with our Creator. That is what we should understand, but it seems it takes us a very, very long time to understand even that one fundamental truth, that we are part of something far, far greater than ourselves, but it takes this being away from that source that gives us the realisation that we are not yet complete, and that this yearning to be back where we know we belong is what drives us ever forward!

Unfortunately it seems to take us many life times to realise this, but when we do, then we know that we are on the road back to our home, our real home that we can then appreciate and understand why we had to leave it in the first place! It may seem a very round about way of getting to where we want to be, but it is this 'round about way' that is what brings about our true self, our Spirit self, the true aspect of the Divine Creator of all life! It may seem like a hard way that we have to go to learn that truth, but it is the only way that awakens what lies dormant within our Spirit self. Once we begin to accept that we are more than this mortal body, then our lessons upon this lower plane are nearly over and we can then look forward to our real life that awaits us, where we can see ourselves as we really are how we have become, through all the trials and tribulations that we have had to endure upon the Earthplane! But the prize that is within our grasp is the one to which we all aspire to! Back, back to where we belong but this time knowing why it was that we had to leave it, only to return, and this time aware of who we are or rather who we have become! And now starts our upward journey through all the spirit realms towards the Godhead and with each new round of lives we become more and more what we are intended to be, one day to be co-workers with those on High, helping those of life experiences, travelling down to the Earthplane in search of who they really are, so that one day they too will return with more understanding of the 'why of life'

76

Chapter 34

We have watched your thoughts and felt that you would like to understand more about electricity and its uses and shall we also say its abuses! No not necessarily intentional but the results can sometimes be quite catastrophic when Electricity is allowed to "go its own way!"

Just about everything in the Universe and the worlds and planets that are housed within it are all controlled by that dynamic force! Even we, that is all of us regardless of what sphere we may be on are governed by that electrical force for in reality is not only electrical force it is "life force!" Bodies are made up of all forms of electrical currents and impulses both negative and positive! You just cannot get away from their influence! You know yourself from your own observation that when you meet certain people you either feel an affinity with them or perhaps just the opposite and you cannot quite put your finger on why that is! Well of course it is all to do with your electric field of life force that surrounds you on a permanent basis! For without these life giving currents you would just be an "inanimate shell" do you follow what we are saying? We, that's we who dwell in the Spirit world are "made up" of far more electrical impulses than you upon the Earthplane! Your dense atmosphere seems to prohibit you getting all of the necessary electrical "molecules" that your body really needs. That is why you have to supplement it with heavy food substances. Fortunately we do not need that form of sustenance! We live and thrive through our electrical intake which is literally "our life food!" though we do have other forms of food if and when we wish it, but that is all regulated as it were by thought which of course is activated by, yes, electricity! There is no getting away from it is there? Thought, that is the Mind that controls that power is like a little power house of electricity! Nothing can be achieved without that force, it is everywhere, in the Earth, the Sky, yes even in the oceans that lap the shores of your continents! We, that is all of us and I suppose I should include all of the so called living creations and yes even those objects that you like to call "inanimate." They too have a field of electric life force surrounding and also within them! Like we all have, only with those so called "inanimate's" the electrical force, shall we say "slumbers" if you can get our meaning! While with all other living creations this force is forever alive and active and that little Brother includes the very ground that you walk upon! Do you not have what is known as "Ley lines," forces that exist in vast quantities, but not always understood although some people do have the ability to tap into this dormant energy! There is so much that Man has yet to learn and come to terms with this life giving force, for it will be to his advantage ultimately. That is when he has studied the structure of it's mechanics! We are able with our advanced thought power to manipulate electrical impulses and currents for our own use! We use electricity as a "tool" but only when we have been shown how to and not before! In the wrong hand's it can become unstable, volatile and destructive and yes very, very dangerous! Just look at what destructive powers it can unleash with Tornadoes, lightening strikes, tidal waves and volcanic eruptions to name but just a few, but let me hasten to add these phenomena only apply to your Earthplane! On other planets and worlds the effects can be somewhat different! That is not to say lesser but somehow their structures react in a different way because of their locality in the Universe! That will make you think my friend! You see all "parts" of the Universe do not behave in the same manner! Some parts are shall we say in a fluid state of "reconstruction" and yes even of a form of "deconstruction." In other words they become amalgamated with a similar part, so becoming even more forceful! The Universe is a living, vibrating, extension of what you upon Earth term the "Breath of the Almighty Creator" in other words God! I would like to have added, one of them! but I feel that would not "go down" very well with some of your more orthodox readers! You I know understand what has been hinted at! Thank goodness for an open mind!

So now you can appreciate just how complex and vast is this ongoing "experimentation" of not only your known Universe but all of the others that at present dwell only in the minds of your "fiction writers" but which are the realities if they only knew it! And that also goes for the humanities, the human body is a wonderful mechanism, capable of so much more than man is aware of at present! In time he will learn and know how the hidden mysteries of his body can be used, but not yet! Not yet! He has yet to learn how to control his emotions which stem from his thoughts mechanism, The Mind and all that that implies! Regeneration of parts of the body that have become diseased is what we are talking about! But that form of creative ability is not in the foreseeable future. Though the Scientists on our side of life have perfected this ability with what you might call "human guinea pigs" those who have volunteered for this form of experimentation, we do not wish or rather we are not allowed to pursue that part of this discourse!

Suffice to say that one day, it will be used upon your Earthplane, when you have proved that you are able to not only cope with it, but use it freely for the good of all and not for the few who have the money to pay for it! For there will be so called clinics. There we have been told to stop right there! So we must!

This talk about Electricity and its uses is a vast subject and one that we will come back to in due course that we promise you.

Chapter 35

Further to our discussion the other day regarding Electricity and it's uses! We will continue with that theme. As you already know all living matter has an electrical force field of energy not only surrounding it but also penetrating it and that goes especially for what we will term the human body and believe us that also includes us upon your so called Spirit plane! For we still consider ourselves as human beings, for that is what we are just an extension of the human body that has dwelt upon the Earthplane! You understand what we are implying? Our world, which is also yours when you vacate the lower one, is made up primarily of electrical wavelengths, molecules, electric vapours and many more that you upon the Earthplane know nothing about! We, that is when we transfer from the earth to this realm are taught how we can use this living force for our own use! It does not come automatically, for electricity is a very potent tool when you know how it can be "harnessed" and tamed as it were! For the electrical currents are literally everywhere, as they are upon your planet, only because of the denseness of your surroundings you cannot always observe it, but nevertheless it does exist and in abundance! In time you will learn how to use this form of power for many things, including a new form of "transport" which will require no moving parts as in your engines, for the motivation will come from Electrical wavelengths, that will propel your vehicles along! No noise, no pollution! But that I am afraid is a very long way off for you upon the Earth!

We do have forms of transportation, but nothing is as crude as your vehicles that you have to use to get you to where you wish to go to! We use a form of magnetic beam that we, shall we say, plug into and that is all that is needed! Difficult for you to understand the procedure, but believe us it does work and there is absolutely no form of accidents that could possibly occur! The same principle is applied to our form of sky transport. But that is another subject!

Now you have wondered in your thoughts just what so called Spirit body is made of haven't you? Well we are solid when we wish to be and that is on a permanent basis when we are on our realm, we don't keep appearing and disappearing, we are quite normal believe us! Though probably to you our normality would seem rather wonderful, but then you would be looking at it from a physical viewpoint which could not take in what to us is normal reality! Such a lot for you to learn when you do come over to us isn't there? It truly is a New Life in every way! Now to continue, with what to put in your language is our bodily components!

As you are aware we do not require your form of solid food and liquid to sustain our life force! We are as we have said, made up of electrical substance, which we can manipulate how we wish by Thought and for the sake of argument, we assume a physical form of identity for all normal purposes, if we intend to be "seen" (and that is a loose term) by those upon a lower sphere than ours. For example, your Earthplane, we assume, how can we put it? We remain is a more appropriate word, we remain as a physical form of identity, but in reality it is not our normal form of solidity! We send by thought emanation a replica of ourselves that to all intents and purposes is the real one! Acting and speaking as we normally do, so that whoever it is that is observing us does not know the difference. We are to all intents and purposes there in the 'flesh' so to speak! We, that is the real one, has absolute authority over our other self and we know and experience everything that, that other one is going through! Difficult perhaps for you to quite understand, but that is one way that we can be in two places at once! More for you to learn when you are with us! Now all of this shall we say 'phenomena' is controlled by Electricity to put it simply! We can even be a part of you when we want to and all through electrical currents and wavelengths! We start by knowing your particular 'wavelength' that is your basic make up. We can then, as it were, lock on to that wavelength and so we can appreciate all your feelings and mental make up! Though we do not influence your thought pattern unless we have your prior permission to do so! And that of course is done through thought as well! We can be around you without your actually being aware of us and this too is done through thought waves of electrical light substance, that is why you are sometimes aware of light emanations either outwardly or within your inner perception! You can now see that all forms of electrical discharges are of a very creative nature when properly understood! And we have only touched the fringe of its capabilities! If you could view with your naked eye you would see millions and millions of little light emanations that make up your atmosphere, they are 'life forms' in action, so you can now understand why it is that some people are affected by those electrical gadgets that you have around your home! In fact some people even have an adverse effect upon these objects, that is why they always seem to be going wrong!

Fortunately we know how to control our life force and so we are not affected in any way adversely. We will take you even further in another discourse, but for the present we feel we will leave it there and let you ponder upon what has been written.